COMMUNITY
AND
SCHOOLS

Promise and Paradox

COMMUNITY
AND
SCHOOLS
Promise and Paradox

Carol Merz and Gail C. Furman

Foreword by William P. Foster

Teachers College, Columbia University
New York and London

To our children
Ruth and Sarah, Joshua and Leah

who have taught us the meaning of community of kinship

Published by Teachers College Press, 1234 Amsterdam Avenue, New York, NY 10027

Library of Congress Cataloging-in-Publication Data

Merz, Carol.
    Community and schools : promise and paradox / Carol Merz & Gail
  Furman.
      p. cm.
  Includes bibliographical references (p.) and index.
  ISBN 0-8077-3617-1 (alk. paper). — ISBN 0-8077-3616-3 (pbk.)
    1. Community and school—United States.   2. School environment—
United States.   3. Educational sociology—United States.
  4. Educational change—United States.   I. Furman, Gail.   II. Title.
LC221.M47   1997
371.19—dc21   96-50968

ISBN 0-8077-3616-3 (paper)
ISBN 0-8077-3617-1 (cloth)

Printed on acid-free paper
Manufactured in the United States of America

04 03 02 01 00 99 98 97   8 7 6 5 4 3 2 1

Contents

Foreword

The concept of "community" has a particular attraction for many of us; it will often lead to flights of nostalgic fancy, suggesting a simpler and more meaningful way of being where the complexities of modernity are reduced to manageable issues. It reminds us of those ties that are lifelong bonds, those memories of a past constructed around obligation, commitment, and mutual assistance. This community is a community of longing, driven by remembrance.

Such communities may never have existed as we re-create them in our collective memory, but they nevertheless stand as possibilities for us. There are some notable characteristics of the modern world that urge us to return to simpler times: The world as we know it is fragmented and fractured; it is dominated by economic and regulatory institutions over which there seems to be little control; its success depends on what has been labeled a possessive individualism; and it reflects a public life in some disarray.

The fragmentation comes from the artificial disruption of the rhythms of nature and from the imposition of structures of division, so that family life is separated from work life, from school life, from leisure, and so on. Fragmentation also occurs when conflicting values bump against each other, and when the diverse traditions of a pluralist and multicultural society are not each fully respected. Economic (and in particular consumerist) institutions control homes and jobs, and regulatory institutions (including regional and national bureaucratic agencies) shape our education, control our wages, and govern our mores.

We feed such institutions by viewing ourselves as individual consumers whose public obligations are defined contractually and not always with respect to compelling moral choices. Achievement, status, prestige, and other signs of social success are largely individual accomplishments, and the rewards so attained are individually distributed. For so many of us, it is the rewards, materialistic and consumable, that make the contest worth playing. This individualism, fueled by desire, has its toll on public life as well. Public leadership is often a leadership of transaction, a leadership of exchanges, and too often such leadership conducts its business with neither public knowledge nor consent.

The picture painted is extreme, but it does reflect tendencies in the modern state to raise personal autonomy and institutional economics above the bonds of church and family; it reflects the needs of a society driven by the production function; it reflects a social division where the private sphere is the major forum in which values and morals can be debated and discussed. Yet, even against such a background, the ideas of community and communal association remain, and often remain strong. How then does community survive, and how might it be nurtured? This is the question addressed by Carol Merz and Gail C. Furman.

In this book, the authors present an argument on community in schools based on sociological theory as well as on their own social analysis. They have produced a realistic and thought-provoking work that is theoretically sound yet practically based. Moving beyond the mere rhetoric of community, they offer analysis; to show how the achievement of community in schools is necessary but not easy. Starting with the classical sociological distinction between *Gesellschaft* and *Gemeinschaft*, which I would roughly translate as the distinction between "society" (based on rules) and "community" (based on affect), the authors review current scholarship on the idea of community. Indeed, though much has been written on this topic in the last several years, not until this book has there been such an intensive effort to present a realistic appraisal of the notion of community, to discuss actual programs aimed at community building, and to evaluate and assess the possibilities of re-establishing community in schools in our time.

There are several important points in this book that make it particularly useful for educators concerned with the development of social environments that stress nurturance over control. First, the authors show that the establishment of community in schools is possible, but attempts that only try to re-create the past will not work. The demands of the modern world are different from those our ancestors faced, and educators and policy-makers must start with this truth. Hortatory cries aside, the political and economic realities of educating youth in these times require community-builders to adopt a new realism that recognizes some of the conditions of modern life discussed above.

Secondly, the book points to the danger of unanticipated effects; in other words, efforts to establish more meaningful communities in educational settings can sometimes result in more bureaucratic and less personal environments. For example, the authors show how some attempts to make schools more child-responsive and inclusive, to be more community oriented, can result in the addition of more layers of regulation that interfere with the best of intentions. In a similar vein, the authors demonstrate how many attempts to "package" community building through the programmatic efforts of nationally recognized educators ignore the spirit of the local; as a result, they may simply impose more demands on teachers and pupils alike, and thereby contribute to their alienation from community.

Perhaps the most important contribution of this fine volume is the authors' analysis of the potential for the creation of viable and meaningful community in schools. They show it can be done and that some schools are doing it. They also show a strong and often unsurfaced anti-communitarian ethos exists in our school systems, one in which schools are considered instruments: instruments of the economy, so that literate and productive workers are prepared; instruments of the state, so that laws are followed willingly; instruments of bureaucracy, so that teachers and other educational officials remain employed. The idea that schools should just be is an idea foreign to a pragmatic culture. Dewey made this same observation many years ago but many of us still fail to see that schools are about life, not preparation for life.

Thus this text provides valuable lessons for those educators who take seriously the values of caring, neighborliness, friendship, and respect, and who wish to incorporate such values in a systemic fashion that contributes to the formation of both academic and political consciousness. One lesson might be for us to be aware and awake. This means that we need to be conscious of the impositions large systems make into personal and communal spaces, thereby depriving us of choice. In the process of schooling, state mandates, regulatory bodies, and other well-intentioned attempts at control can be so intrusive.

A second lesson might be to consider the politics of resistance. By being awake and aware, we can observe the tendency toward conformity that large systems impose, tendencies that need to be resisted. Such resistance may be nothing more than alerting a neighbor, or it may involve a determined and coordinated effort to involve a community, a parent group, or a group of students and teachers in the determination of the educational process most appropriate for their situation.

Another lesson we can draw from this work is the value of lightening up. A visit to many schools that have successfully established a sense of community will show an ordered chaos; much like the greater community of which it is a part, such school communities will have children with different values, different needs, and different ways of

ordering their lives. But all are respected, and all are expected to contribute to the principles of self-governance, caring, and work. While
the orderliness so much desired in institutional settings is often missing in these schools, it is replaced by a dynamism that is self-generated
by eager minds.

Thus, Merz and Furman have provided us with serious analysis on
the meaning of community in schools, an analysis that is founded in
sociological theory but goes further by providing practical examples of
the successes and failures of community-building efforts. Their analysis suggests both caution and hope: Caution is required because the
regulatory and conformist tendencies of large systems in modern life
can impede—indeed, strangle—any efforts that we bring to the creation of community. Hope, though, is necessary, because such environments do exist, and exist as meaningful alternatives to a rigor-
bound system. Even if it did nothing else, this book would show us the
pitfalls and the possibilities of community building. Eschewing the
sermon-like quality of so much that is written in this area, the authors
offer the reader an examination of community that is crafted with
precision, yet ultimately allows the reader to rekindle the flame of
caring for each other in meaningful ways.

William P. Foster
Indiana University

1

The Dilemma of Community

Whatever the future may have in store, one thing is certain.
Unless local communal life can be restored, the public can-
not adequately resolve its most urgent problem: to find and
identify itself.
— *Dewey*, The Public and Its Problems

The longing for a sense of community, expressed by John Dewey so many years ago, has become a major theme in recent writings about educational and social issues. We seem to have a national sense of loss for the neighborhoods in which we grew up, whether or not they were as cohesive and comfortable as we characterize them in our memories. We see our lives becoming increasingly fragmented, if not chaotic, and long for a simpler life in which order was assumed. Specialization has made our lives socially and geographically dispersed as we work, learn, shop, play, and worship in unrelated places with unrelated groups of people. Today in schools, whether we are students, teachers, parents, administrators, or board members, we find ourselves disenchanted with an impersonal bureaucracy, yet the complexity of our work leads us to find bureaucratic and technological ways of working. People's need for a cohesive, identifiable community and their frustration with bureaucracy lie at the heart of many late 20th century school reforms. Schools must serve a wide range of people—students, parents, teachers, and future employers of students, to name a few; we must decide whether it is possible to create schools today that can serve this wide range of people and give them confidence that they are recognized as individuals or whether the complexity of our world requires bureaucracies in which people are interchangeable within defined roles.

Disenchantment with bureaucracy is not a new phenomenon nor is nostalgia for a simpler life. In fact, tension between the need for increased organization and the need for greater individuality and intimacy has played an important role in social history since the industrial revolution. An early example is Charles Dickens's *Hard Times* (1854/1989) in which he compares the cold, rational, industrial world of the

1

Gradgrinds with the more intimate, emotional, warmer relationships of Sleary's circus. The novel is set in the English midlands, where industrial life became particularly grim and the profits of the factory owners took a severe toll on the lives of the workers and their families. Dickens points out how meager and regimented the workers' lives are compared with the lives of traveling circus people. The circus is an interesting analogy because it symbolizes fantasy and frivolity. Even though the circus workers face danger, financial insecurity, and peculiar relationships, they work as a family, accepting and supporting one another. They are able to sell their skills to the public while moving from meadow to meadow and setting up decorative tents, the antithesis of the smoke-belching factory.

Today it is widely assumed that communities and neighborhoods are in decline and no longer serve the important social roles they once did. Most specifically for the schools, the community at large no longer seems to serve a socializing role for youth. At one time, the schools were simply one of a number of institutions, including the church, extended families, and interrelated patterns of friendship and commerce, that taught children how to live as adults. Today, many adults in schools see themselves as bearing more and more of that responsibility alone. Moreover, as communities have become more diverse, it has been increasingly difficult for schools to define an educational program that will meet the needs of all the children in the community effectively.

Our lives have changed dramatically in the late 20th century. Communication technology and efficient transportation allow us to maintain ties with people at great distances. Few of us work in the same neighborhood where we live. Most of us have lived in several different places, and our lives have been shaped by a number of forces, so we tend to find stores, restaurants, churches, and entertainment that cater to our tastes, often some distance from our homes. We form networks of friends with similar tastes and experiences, but these friends are rarely our neighbors. Our increased mobility means we often have little common history with our local friends, and those friends and relatives with whom we have a common history are usually at a distance great enough that we don't encounter them incidentally in our lives.

We live in a very complicated world that requires increasing specialization. Few of us have the same job our parents did, or if we do have basically the same job, it is probably carried out in a very different place or manner. Setting aside the job of a teacher, which we will deal with specifically later, doctors tend now to work in large organizations, and even family practice is considered a specialty today. Lawyers, bankers, auto mechanics, all practice in a more specialized and technical world. This means that we can no longer live in small, coherent enclaves in which we can each provide a general service and receive all our services without traveling outside. This expanding of our lives geographically through specialization, communication, and transportation has a great impact on our schools.

DEFINITIONS OF COMMUNITY

Our longing for community in a modern world is often expressed in language that is vague and romantic. In many instances we seem to have a nostalgic notion of what community means, and we experience its loss in a generalized sense of loss or lack of belonging (Mitchell, 1990). In the next chapter we will suggest that our thinking about community and its relationship to schools would be greatly enhanced by considering how sociologists have conceptualized community within various theoretical schemata. Sociologists have no universally accepted definition of community; Bender (1978) points out that the concept of community is a fundamental idea in sociology, but its definitions vary widely within the field.

In education, we use the term *community* with many different shades of meaning. In some senses, community means place; it means the connectedness of a geographically identifiable neighborhood. Coleman (1985) writes about neighborhood schools and their place in the fabric of American education. Using the term *functional community*, Coleman describes geographically cohesive communities in which children attend school with the children of their parents' associates, a characteristic he calls *intergenerational closure*. These functional communities are defined by a number of characteristics including place, work, church, recreation, and kinship; the patterns of interaction of children in the schools are parallel to the social interactions among adults in the community. But Coleman points out that while increased mobility in this country has caused the functional community based on residence to disappear, schools continue to be based on residential patterns. Many of the education reforms today attempt to involve parents with the school, bringing groups of parents together to interact. This kind of activity takes a good deal of energy and abundant resources to do what happened naturally in schools serving functional neighborhood communities.

Sometimes educators, particularly administrators, use the term *community* to mean the public, political world external to the school. It is the audience for their public relations campaigns and is usually conceptualized as a mix of opinions and powers that attempt with varying degrees of success to control the schools. Used in this way, community is a descriptive term, and there is no assumption that it has any ideological coherence or unity. In fact, most school systems assume factions in their "communities." They may further complicate the issue by using the term to refer to one of the specific subgroups identified by a belief system or ethnic factor, as in "our Mormon community" or "our Asian community."

Sometimes community means a group of people with shared values. Coleman (1985) gives examples of elite private schools that serve communities that have shared values and intergenerational closure but are not necessarily geographically defined. Schools of choice often attempt to create this type of community by emphasizing a style or theme for their educational program. Religious or church-affiliated schools serve communities defined by shared values and often exhibit intergenerational closure. Coleman points out that schools can reestablish intergenerational closure by being organized around a work site. In fact, some studies of school choice show that parents will often choose schools convenient to their work locations.

Coleman (1987) suggests that families and communities supply "social capital," by which he means a kind of social "know-how" in relationships and norms that is helpful in raising and educating children. Social capital can be developed from contacts in the church, neighborhood, or any social grouping with intergenerational closure. The availability of these sources is especially important for children from families that lack social capital, and the absence of such opportunities today constitutes a serious loss.

Sometimes we use the term *community* to refer to a coherent quality of a school itself (McLaughlin, 1991; Sergiovanni, 1992, 1994). In speaking of school as community, writers talk about relationships within a school as personal, committed, and familial. Some people stress the importance of forging a shared value system to enhance the community aspects of a school. Advocates of these kinds of schools talk about their ability to provide security and identity to students and teachers.

This changing use of the term confuses our thinking about the concept of community. Each use of the term in the definitions discussed above focuses on different attributes of a community. In the next two chapters we will examine some of the important attributes of community, both positive and negative, in an attempt to arrive at a useful set of concepts clustered in the term *community*. In the rest of this chapter we will discuss the school in relation to the term community as applied to an external social setting, an identifiable constituent group, or a quality about the school itself.

SCHOOLS IN RELATIONSHIP TO
THE SURROUNDING COMMUNITY

Schools in America are historically rooted in local, geographically defined communities. In the first settlements, schools were set up and governed by town councils. The school building often served as the community hall, and the boundaries between the school and the community were indistinct. Communities were highly homogeneous, and values were shared widely. The school and its course of study were an extension of the homes, the church, and the commerce of the community. This type of school, labeled by Tyack (1974) a village school, was amazingly durable as an institution; with only minor changes, it served small, homogeneous, isolated communities for about 300 years.

With industrialization, urbanization, and massive immigration at the end of the 19th century and the beginning of the 20th century, big changes occurred in schools. These changes, documented extensively by Cremin (1988) and Tyack (1974), created the modern urban system of schooling, which promises to be almost as durable as the village school. To deal with the task of educating thousands of immigrant and rural children who had little in common, urban schools were set up as efficient organizations to socialize children to be good, productive American citizens. As in the village school, there was a widespread assumption about the role and values of the school. While many of these values were not shared by the families at home, there was little question about the melting-pot philosophy. In fact, in many ways, these schools were established to create a culture that was distinctly different from the culture of the home.

While the success of establishing a school system to accommodate great numbers of children arriving in the rapidly growing cities of America was unprecedented, the system has struggled to accommodate cultural changes in the last half of the 20th century. The very qualities that allowed the system to socialize immigrants to "the American way" prevented the system from responding to individual needs. In the same way that schools representing urban, often ethnic, wards were combined to create an urban school system, schools in small towns across the United States consolidated into increasingly centralized systems. At the same time, an increasingly sophisticated educational technology has allowed school people to see that students need different kinds of education and the national mood has caused people to want different kinds of education. No longer is the melting-pot philosophy unchallenged; people want schools that reflect the diversity of America today.

Many critics of schools say schools have become alienated from the communities they serve, and rebuilding or restoring community ties has become a major theme in educational reform. Some of these reforms go back to the 1960s with various decentralization efforts in large cities. For example, both New York and Chicago established community school boards in an effort to make schools more responsive to local communities. The decentralization movement ultimately became school-based management (SBM), a process almost universally adopted today by which schools retain some decisions previously made by the central board or administration. A representative site council makes various decisions, usually involving some aspects of curriculum, budget, and personnel. Other efforts to involve parents in schools came with the extensively funded federal programs of the 1970s. Most of these programs required the establishment of both a parent education component and a council to give parents a voice in program governance.

Over the years a number of programs have been established to involve parents in the education of their children. One of the first and best known programs of this sort is the one established by James Comer (1988) in which he analyzed many of the supportive elements of his own childhood and attempted to build a similar support system in schools in New Haven. Other programs try to bring modern community influences into the school by involving businesses in the education process. Partnerships with business have become very popular in urban areas, some of the better known being the Boston Compact and the Atlanta Partnership for Business and Education (Clark, 1991). Comer's program will be discussed in relationship to *Gemeinschaft* and *Gesellschaft* in Chapter 6.

As it became clearer that the origins of many educational problems lay outside the schools, more and more reform efforts have been directed at the social problems surrounding the school. Many of these consider community to be something more than neighborhood. Some programs have attempted to deal with the fragmentation that occurs in the lives of "at-risk" students by creating support communities in which educational, social, and health services are combined in one system, just as Comer's (1988) project in New Haven involved parents, teachers, counselors, social workers, and students in a highly coordinated model.

Other reform programs have attempted to simplify the complicated delivery system that comes from separately funded services. *Who Controls Major Federal Programs for Children and Families: Rube Goldberg Revisited* (Dunkle, 1995) examines 76 federal programs for which 88 separate federal agencies have primary responsibility. An example is the New Beginnings Program in San Diego (Melaville & Blank, 1993) in which social and health services are coordinated through the school site. Coordinated-services programs have become very popular with government and granting agencies, where they are seen as highly efficient. Evaluations have yet to show any efficiency in these programs (Crowson & Boyd, 1993), and, in fact, they may be more expensive than separate delivery systems, but they may deliver more services to more clients than would otherwise be possible.

SCHOOLS AS COMMUNITY

Sometimes because of the disconnectedness of life outside the school, and the difficulty of establishing stable relationships with families, schools attempt to create a community within the school itself (Sergiovanni, 1992, 1994). Other reformers concentrate on the relationships among teachers and advocate building "professional communities" of collegial support (McLaughlin, 1991). Still other reformers, in acknowledging the diversity of society today, try to link schools to more homogeneous families through school choice (Alexander, 1993).

Sergiovanni (1994) is one of the foremost among writers who focus on school as community. These see the lack of social and emotional support in children's lives outside the school and attempt to supply some of that support by changing the nature of the school. Sergiovanni bases his discussion of community on the definition from Blau and Scott (1962) of communities as social organizations built on commitment and relationships that lead to interdependencies. The shared values and common purpose of schools allow schools to be communities, according to Sergiovanni. Once schools are established as communities, then the relationships of community make many of the usual management tasks unnecessary—relationships become focused on mutual commitments and obligations rather than on the usual relationships of supervision or contractual agreements. Sergiovanni documents the need for community and explores the possibility of establishing schools as communities in many different ways. His work, and Noddings's (1992) work on caring, emphasizes the emotional dimensions necessary for schools to succeed today.

One variation on the school as community theme examines the needs of teachers in schools, and based on the theory that teachers who are isolated and perhaps alienated cannot teach well, some reformers attempt to build professional communities to support teachers (McLaughlin, 1991). In some senses these programs could be seen as attempting to build the social capital of the school, in Coleman's (1987) terms, before attempting to draw on it for students. While these programs lead to greater teacher satisfaction and could logically be related to better conditions for students, there is little direct evidence that student learning or behavior improves. Studies that show student growth usually include broader definitions of community than the relationships among teachers; these studies will be reviewed in Chapter 6.

In its role as community, the school is really designed to function as a surrogate for the traditional family and the social setting in which it existed. The basis for this role is the assumption that students today often have fragmented home lives and require greater nurturance and stability in the school setting. In Chapter 4 we will examine how the role of the school has changed from being one aspect of a very coherent social setting to today's role in a complex, specialized, even chaotic social setting. Programs that attempt to create school as community also lead to an interesting set of questions regarding establishing community-like relationships within the workplace. We will return to this question in subsequent discussions of definitions of community and discussions of new ways in which people attempt to meet the needs for community in a highly complex and structured world.

CRITICISMS OF COMMUNITY-BASED REFORMS: EXPANDING BUREAUCRACY

Most of the criticisms of school reform have not been on theoretical grounds. Most have simply pointed out that not much has changed (Cuban, 1988; Sarason, 1982; Tyack, 1990). Critics have pointed out again and again that the American school is a very durable institution. While changes can be made in some places at some times, the inertia of the system tends to restore it to its original condition. Writers see great hope in small-scale reform related to a specific client community, but the reforms don't seem to move to other sites very well, and seem to generalize to larger-scale implementations even less well. This may tell us more about the role of community than it does about educational techniques.

Increasing bureaucracy has been a frequent, although often unintentional, response to the problems plaguing the schools in late 20th century America. It seems that bureaucratic solutions can be counterproductive when used to solve problems stemming from loss of community, although few writers discuss appropriate pairing of these concepts. Mitchell (1990) is one of the few exceptions, as he identifies a widespread sense of loss, in general, as one of the major challenges to schools in the 19th and 20th centuries. Mitchell writes that dilemmas in modern life are caused by three factors: "loss," as a natural concomitant of change; "belonging," as the way people relate to each other; and "becoming," as the way we prepare for our future. While he does not identify the community as a concept in these discussions, it is inherent in his discussion of belonging, being one of the traditional ways people established their sense of belonging.

Mitchell (1990) describes the school as a tool society has devised for dealing with these underlying issues, and schools have been charged with the task of "repairing debilitating loss, creating the right forms of belonging and creating an acceptable sense of becoming" (p. 21). But these tasks have never been the overt, or sole, work of the school, nor has the school been the sole institution attempting to deal with these issues. Typically schools have attempted to deal with loss by creating greater order, such as hiring more administrators and instituting new procedures. These measures are often undertaken in reaction to the public's fear that schools have lost control; aware that people feel insecure as they experience loss, schools have increased control and authority in an attempt to make people feel more secure. Mitchell sees this activity, which inevitably increases the bureaucracy of schools, as essentially misguided. He advocates that schools should accept loss as a natural part of human existence, and direct their efforts instead to increasing belonging. Relying on classic sociology and anthropology, Mitchell points out that people get a sense of belonging from identifying with a group, often defined by place, kinship, or ethnicity. Although bureaucracies were created to give people clearly identified roles in large groups, they do not serve the same ends as earlier social groupings. Quoting anthropologists, Mitchell again points out that teachers in many of today's high schools encounter more students in one day than the number of people who lived in a whole tribal village. Thus bureaucratic attempts to increase physical or psychological security, while apparently addressing loss, can exacerbate the problems of belonging by creating an atmosphere that is increasingly impersonal. In Chapter 3 we will explore what community might mean in today's world.

CONCLUSION

The education world seems generally unaware that its responses to the loss of community have been to create ever more specialized and complex systems, which are, by definition, bureaucracies. Historically, bureaucracies have been the answer to many of the school's problems but have created a set of other problems, which are becoming increasingly acute. In general, people are becoming more and more disenchanted with bureaucracies today, and while we still value efficiency, we long for a more personal connection to the world in which we live. Increased specialization has caused the schools to focus on the educational function while the social needs of children have increased. The varying concepts of community are used frequently in discussions of these problems and in proposals to address them.

While the way that each current reform writer has looked at community is useful, each is limited in that it addresses only a narrow range of community attributes and fails to address a broader, more profound need for human linkages. These writers share a certain naiveté in assuming that identifying and providing one or two of the attributes of community will satisfy this need. They fail to address the complexity of interrelated attributes of community or how modern schools may deal with our inability to meet all of these aspects of this basic human need.

In many cases, the concept of community is not theoretically clear:

- What do we mean by community?
- What constitutes a community in late 20th century America?
- What is the school's place or role in relation to this community?
- Should this role be modified to meet the needs produced by a community in "decline"?
- How do specific reform proposals, such as interagency collaboration or school-based management, fit with the concepts of community and the role of the schools in relation to community?
- Can the school create authentic linkages with communities as they now exist?

In this book we are interested in developing a framework for understanding the concepts of community and bureaucracy, as developed through sociological theory, in a way that may be useful to educators. In Chapter 2 we examine classical sociological theory of community that may be applied to schools today. In Chapter 3, we look at more contemporary interpretations of community, including feminist theory and the modern communitarian movement, in an attempt to develop a framework that will work realistically for modern life. In Chapter 4 we analyze the changing relationship of schools to the external world, and specifically examine the changing role of the teacher. In Chapters 5 and 6, we analyze specific school reform policies and proposals in light of the community framework we develop; in Chapter 5 we look at reforms intended to build closer connections between schools and their external communities; in Chapter 6 we examine reforms intended to create schools as communities. Throughout this discussion, we use the term *school* in a generic sense, to mean state-run, K–12 public schools in a traditional governance model. While we recognize that community issues differ in some ways across the elementary and secondary levels, the major themes we discuss apply to both levels. Further, most of our analysis is more applicable to larger school systems in urban areas than to rural schools, which continue to retain stronger ties to their local communities. Indeed, as we will see in Chapters 5 and 6, most reforms aimed at school-community connections or at the school as community have been proposed for these larger schools. Finally, in Chapter 7, we suggest ways in which more useful linkages may be developed between the schools and community, and between individuals in the schools. It is our ultimate hope that we can clarify what people need to experience in order to achieve a sense of community, with the knowledge of the cost and feasibility of achieving that experience today.

2

Theory of Community:
Gemeinschaft and *Gesellschaft*

All intimate, private, and exclusive living together, so we discover, is understood as life in Gemeinschaft. Gesellschaft *is public life—it is the world itself. In* Gemeinschaft *with one's family, one lives from birth on, bound in weal and woe. One goes into* Gesellschaft *as one goes into a strange country.*
— *Tönnies*, Community and Society

The concept of community was a central concern of several 19th-century social theorists, including Tönnies, Weber, and Durkheim. With society caught up in rapid industrialization and urbanization, these early sociologists were concerned with the potential disintegration of the traditional pattern of social life. Given the dated context of this early work, and problems of translation from the German, it may seem inaccessible and anachronistic to educators concerned with the year 2000. Yet this work on the theory of community, first and perhaps most clearly articulated by Tönnies (1887/1957), offers a useful framework for understanding community and the school's role in community.

The central idea of Tönnies (1887/1957) system of understanding social relationships is the *Gemeinschaft/Gesellschaft* continuum. A good deal of modern social theory has grown out of this typology; according to Bender (1978), it is "one of the discipline's most enduring and fruitful concepts for studying social change" (p. 17). *Gemeinschaft* and *Gesellschaft* are loosely translated into English as "community" and "society," but in discussions of theory, they usually appear in their original German since they do not translate exactly. We will continue to use the German terms in the hope that we retain greater precision and fidelity in discussing Tönnies work. We will also use the adjective forms, *gemeinschaftlich* and *gesellschaftlich*, since there seem to be no appropriate English alternatives.

Gemeinschaft and *Gesellschaft* are mentioned increasingly in the education literature regarding community (Crowson, 1992; Crowson & Boyd, 1993; Lutz & Iannacone, 1978; Lutz & Merz, 1992; Sergiovanni, 1994). Recent computer searches of sociological databases turn up 70–80 current uses of the terms, indicating that writers are finding these concepts useful in analyzing modern community problems. We think that before adopting the terms as our own, it is worthwhile to return to the original literature, to examine the original meanings, and to look at the way the terms have been considered by others.

DEVELOPMENT OF THE CONCEPTS

Ferdinand Tönnies was a German sociologist born in 1855 in Schleswig-Holstein to a prosperous farming family. He studied philosophy, history, and economics at several German universities, receiving his doctorate from Tübingen in 1877. He published *Gemeinschaft und Gesellschaft*, the work for which he is best known, in 1887 at the age of 32; he became a professor at the University of Kiel that same year. He, with Georg Simmel, Max Weber, and others, founded the German Society for Sociology. Increasingly concerned with the Nazi movement, he joined the Social Democratic Party in 1932, wrote a number of anti-Nazi articles, and was summarily dismissed from his academic position by the Nazi regime in 1933. He died in 1936.

As did other early sociologists, Tönnies established an ideal-typical continuum to describe social relationships. Polar ends of the continuum are commonly misconstrued to represent two kinds of real situations, whereas in fact Tönnies intended that they be considered ideal concepts, describing aspects of all social relationships. He wrote that all human relationships have aspects of each in varying degrees.

Gemeinschaft represented the traditional folk relationships, based on common locale, kinship, and friendship; such relationships are generally involuntary and functionally diffuse. The most *gemeinschaftlich* relationship, according to Tönnies, is that of mother and child, being an extension of instinct; similarly, the relationship of husband and wife and the relationship among siblings are highly *gemeinschaftlich*. Tönnies wrote that behavior in *Gemeinschaft* is based in natural will in associations built on the family, the tribe, and other social groupings in which people have lived since primitive times. Commitments between people in *Gemeinschaft* are taken for granted, rather than intentionally chosen. In fact, lack of choice is one of the hallmarks of *Gemeinschaft*, and people have often complained of feeling "stuck" in traditional small towns and villages.

Tönnies enumerated three kinds of *Gemeinschaft*: *Gemeinschaft* of blood (kinship), of place (neighborhood), and of mind (friendship). He placed the three types in order of decreasing ability to bind individuals. Thus, the bonds of kinship are strongest and bind people despite separations of time and distance. The bonds of neighborhood can survive periods of separation, but need "to be supported . . . by well defined habits of reunion and sacred customs" (p. 43). Finally, most fragile is "*Gemeinschaft* of mind" or friendship. Tönnies thought that this type was most likely among people who shared a craft or a faith and needed to be "maintained through easy and frequent meetings" (p. 43). Thus Tönnies saw a range of types of *Gemeinschaft*, including the more voluntary, less instinctive, "community of mind," which may have greater relevance today.

The traditional *Gemeinschaft* is ethnically homogeneous. There is little geographic or social mobility in *Gemeinschaft*, so people tend to live out their lives in the position to which they are born; their position is unique, being determined by family and individual characteristics. People know everyone well within their own social span, so people are highly differentiated, or seen to be unique. Relationships are characterized as diffuse in *Gemeinschaft*, that is, people conduct all aspects of their lives—social, business, religious—with the same people. However, because there is often little social interaction or experience with people in other towns, clans, or similar *gemeinschaftlich* groupings, these people may be dealt with stereotypically and not individually differentiated. In fact, the strong ability of a *Gemeinschaft* to give its members a sense of identity may rely to some extent on differentiating its members from members of other groups. There is a strong "we-they" separation in a *Gemeinschaft*.

Gesellschaft represents the public world of commerce, at the other end of Tönnies's continuum, and is organized to meet the demands of the marketplace. Relationships are generally voluntary, based on what Tönnies called rational will, and functionally specific, that is, relating to a certain role or task. These relationships are chosen by the individuals strategically to accomplish some end, or reciprocity, such as commercial trade.

There can be a lot of geographic mobility in a *Gesellschaft* because people move in order to fulfill commercial goals. Social mobility depends theoretically on training and competence, not personal characteristics or family social status, although we will look at other ways in which this often plays out. In many ways, the modern bureaucracy, with its rules, layers of authority, and institutionalized purpose, is the quintessential *Gesellschaft*.

The notion of mutual advantage is important to *Gesellschaft*, and techniques of bargaining and negotiation are *gesellschaftlich* tools. A common definition of community today involves a group with common values that comes together to accomplish a common goal (e.g., Newmann & Wehlage, 1995). Generally the values under discussion relate only to the goal and how it is to be accomplished. This would be a *Gesellschaft*, in Tönnies's schema, not a *Gemeinschaft*, because it hinges on a consciously selected goal.

Weber (1925/1947) incorporated Tönnies's work into his own classification of social relationships: *Kampf* (conflict), *vergemeinschaftung* (translated usually as "communal"), and *vergesellschaftung* (translated as "associative"). Weber saw communal relationships as traditional and based on emotion, such as family or religious groups, but emphasized that even the most associative relationships had communal characteristics, such as the esprit de corp of a military unit. He also emphasized the possibility of coercion and exploitation in communal relationships, citing slavery as the prime example.

Georg Simmel (1903/1950), a contemporary of Tönnies, wrote one of the first analyses of the effect of increasing urbanization on mental health. He saw that emphasis on punctuality and mental calculation led to indifference toward and devaluing of the individual: "The individual has become a mere cog in an enormous organization of things and powers which tear from his hands all progress, spirituality, and value in order to transform them from their subjective form into the form of a purely objective life" (p. 422). Simmel saw that the cries of equality and liberty that had freed the individual from repressive bonds of *Gemeinschaft* in the 18th century had now made individuals indistinguishable.

Nowhere is the ambivalence toward urbanization more clearly evident than in the work of Durkheim. In *The Division of Labor in Society* (1984), Durkheim first saw bureaucracy as a natural and desirable evolutionary process in which people took on increasingly specialized roles, similar to organs of the body or parts of a plant assuming specialized functions. He was later to write in *Suicide* (1897/1951) that this same process led to a disconnectedness, alienation, or anomie leading to depression, panic, and increased rates of suicide associated with business life. Durkheim saw even the positive aspects of modern society as destabilizing; as individuals left the security of the family and the village, they could easily become frustrated and confused by the range of possibilities in their lives.

Social impact

ROLE OF THE INDIVIDUAL

In a *Gemeinschaft*, an individual's status is determined by familial and cultural roles; in a *Gesellschaft*, status is determined by the job that person does, based on competency and training as well as the place of the job-role in the organizational hierarchy (i.e., the number of people that person supervises or the financial contribution of that person's role to organizational productivity). Thus a mother would have very high status in a *gemeinschaftlich*, traditional culture because of the relationship and emotional bonding with that person. A *gesellschaftlich* look at the same person would focus on the job she does and call her a "homemaker" or a "working mom," depending on whether she worked outside the home, because having a job title is important in a *Gesellschaft*. Some have gone so far as to calculate the monetary value of the cleaning, cooking, tutoring, nursing, and chauffeuring done by a mother. While interesting, such calculations of monetary value usually seem irrelevant to the definition of a mother's role in most families, because families generally operate on *gemeinshaftlich* principles.

Since a person's role in *Gesellschaft* is determined by function, people who have the same functional role are largely interchangeable. It matters little where or with whom business is transacted, as long as the job gets done. One conducts financial business at interchangeable bank branches, shops at interchangeable supermarkets, and eats at a fast-food restaurant because the product will be exactly like the product at a similar place. The people who work in these establishments are interchangeable as long as they are pleasant and efficient. While one is always pleased to see a familiar face in the course of daily business, anyone requiring personal continuity in these relationships today will surely become dysfunctional. People go to these places because there is a task to be accomplished, and the task is of much greater importance than the social connectedness that may be experienced.

Relationships in *Gemeinschaft* tend to encompass overlapping and diffuse roles, whereas in *Gesellschaft* they tend to be role-specific. For example, in a traditional village, people knew the doctor, the grocer, the teacher, and the minister socially and saw them engaged in a range of activities. Gossip or village news was exchanged in stores, in churches, in lodges, and in any of the frequent social encounters. In *Gesellschaft*, people rarely see their doctor, their attorney, their child's teacher, or their clergy socially, nor do they encounter these people casually in daily lives, unless they are specifically sought.

Because of the patterns of social contacts, information flows in

Flow of Information

very different ways in *Gemeinschaft* and *Gesellschaft*. In *Gemeinschaft*, information about other people was shared widely because everyone knew the subject of the latest gossip. This quality had obvious drawbacks, in that there was little privacy and people had to live their cultural role all the time. In our more *gesellschaftlich* world of today, clergy and teachers express relief at being able to have a social life in circles other than their parishoners or the parents of their students. Yet this freedom can come at the price of isolation. One is shocked to learn of the death of a friend or neighbor by reading the obituary in a newspaper. In *Gesellschaft* intentional networks must be set up to exchange the information that flowed freely in a village. In typically *gesellschaftlich* fashion, the most frequent occasion for such "networking" is when one seeks a new job or wants to attract new clients.

Villages were good at social monitoring because each person's behavior was visible; misdeeds were hard to hide. It was equally hard for institutions to hide their deviations from the norm, as the members had constant access to each other and could exchange observations and information. Financial misdeeds were obvious, if a leader of an institution exhibited any new unexplained wealth; and new curriculum or treatment of a student in a school would be discussed at length in the community.

Coleman (1985) addresses a specific aspect of the role-diffuse character of *Gemeinschaft* when he discusses intergenerational closure in functional communities. Whereas in *Gemeinschaft*, parents and children had friends among the same families, in *Gesellschaft* each generation has its own set of social and business relationships. *Gesellchaftlich* cultures are set up to carry out commercial tasks and become age-segregated; this has serious implications for schools, as Coleman points out. Schools are usually set up to serve a geographically cohesive neighborhood, but families living in that neighborhood often have few other connections. Information about school is not shared readily among families, nor do parents informally discuss what they would like to see the school do. The school cannot be an expression of values of the neighborhood community when it ceases to function as a community.

Society, without intergenerational closure, ceases to carry out the social monitoring role for the school. Today's high schools are complicated and specialized organizations, with teachers and students encountering between 100 and 200 other people each day. This leads to a great deal of anonymity for students and may be responsible in large part for many problems in schools (Bryk & Driscoll, 1988; Johnson, 1990; Mitchell, 1990; Walberg & Walberg, 1994). Today, parents hear

accountability of students

of their children's misdeeds from school officials, whereas in *Gemeinschaft*, they would hear about them immediately through informal channels. The knowledge that parents and grandparents would know about students' behavior and would be embarrassed in their own social circles was an important social control in villages.

CHOICE AND WILL

In *Gemeinschaft*, a person had little choice; roles and relationships were determined either culturally or biologically. Tönnies (1887/1957) called this factor, which governed most of life in *Gemeinschaft*, "natural will." People did not choose a community, they were born into it. They were generally not free to choose their religion, where they lived, or their circle of friends. Just as they did not choose the families into which they were born, their choice of spouse was limited, and once they were married, they could not choose to leave.

Today in our *gesellschaftlich* world, there is virtually no aspect of life that is not subject to choice. Even relationships between parents and their offspring are subject to choice in terms of frequency and duration of contact. One can even choose to have others care for family members who are dependent, such as small children or elderly parents. In *Gesellschaft*, choices are made on the basis of rational will. People make strategic choices, choosing the option that will be most beneficial based on a rational calculation of advantages and disadvantages. This does not have to be exploitative, although there is certainly a possibility for such. In *Gesellschaft*, solutions can be negotiated to assure that they are advantageous to both parties. Decision making becomes a fine art, an analysis of the many factors to arrive at a decision that will maximize the interests of all parties. Even when a decision must be made for others, as in medical or care-taking decisions for children or disabled persons, the normative decision is rational, based on weighing all the factors, possibly including emotional factors.

This multiplicity of choice can lead to a certain amount of uncertainty, as pointed out early on by Durkheim (1897/1951). It also can be enhanced or limited by the resources available to an individual, thus possibly exacerbating the differences among social classes. Cornell West (1993) writes extensively about the social despair in black America because of the inevitability of the bleakness and poverty of their lives. There is no question that people with more social and economic resources have greater choices, and as choices are exercised, the differences become greater.

THE CONTINUUM

Because this continuum was developed during a time of rapid urban growth, it came to be understood as a process that always moved from small community to larger society. The continuum became simplistic and linear, predicting inevitable loss of *gemeinshaftlich* qualities in relationships, or said more directly, inevitable decline in community. For example, Wirth, in "Urbanism as Way of Life" (1938/1970), saw that population density and social heterogeneity in cities created a life of many superficial or narrow social relationships, devoid of sentiment and characterized by aggrandizement and exploitation.

Progressivism, a social movement in the early part of this century, reacted to increasing bureaucracy by trying to restore small-town life in an industrial world. Jane Addams, John Dewey, and others saw democracy and education as the way to the Great Community. They believed that a well-educated population, with good forms of communication, could establish the same kinds of mutual responsibility on a large scale as that found in small communities. Readers interested in this communitarian movement are directed to Quandt's account in *From Small Town to the Great Community* (1970).

The idea that *gemeinschaftlich* and *gesellschaftlich* qualities could coexist in cultures was asserted by Redfield (1941, 1950) after studying several different cultures. He at first espoused a linear, evolutionary model in which folkways were gradually replaced by urban life styles. His work came under intense criticism from Oscar Lewis (1951) who studied one of the villages in the Yucatan where Redfield had developed his theory. Lewis found that folkways persisted in various aspects of life, regardless of how urbanized the village had become. In response to Lewis's criticism, Redfield (1955) returned to Tönnies' original work and modified his theory, asserting that *gemeinschaftlich* and *gesellschaftlich* qualities were not mutually exclusive or sequential, nor did they lead necessarily to the elimination of folkways. Redfield now saw *Gemeinschaft/Gesellschaft* as an analytic system for describing qualities of human interaction, rather than as a continuum or a sequential system.

Similarly, Gans (1962) questioned Wirth's (1938/1970) interpretation of the city as being automatically *Gesellschaft*. He classified New York City residents into five categories, some of whom lived in very traditional communities. Gans saw the relative degree of isolation and impersonalization of urban life as being determined by socioeconomic status, ethnicity, and life-cycle stage rather than by the qualities of the city itself. He found suburban life to be much more homogeneous and detached than urban life, primarily because of the characteristics of the people who chose to live in the suburbs. In studying networks, Fischer (1982) also found that urban dwellers had as many friendships as rural residents, but they tended to be drawn from wider, more voluntary, circles and to be based less on kinship and other traditional ties. Like Gans, he found that association patterns depended more on personal characteristics of the individuals, such as religion, ethnicity, and level of education, rather than urban or rural setting. He also found that urban dwellers had fewer friends who knew each other. Fischer suggests that the population density of the city allows people to find others with similar interests, especially others sharing the individual's primary interest. Thus it is possible that urban friendships are more single-purpose and less generalized than friendships of rural people, hence less *gemeinschaftlich.*

Following these reconsiderations of *Gemeinschaft* and *Gesellschaft*, Bender (1978) called for a "perspective that will enable us to take an overview of the simultaneous polarity and reciprocity of these two patterns of human interaction" (p. 43). Using this perspective, he traced the history of community in America and found "crisis and confusion in American social thought" (p. 144) based on a deep nostalgia for the comfortable, familiar community in the face of increasingly complex social organization. Bender asserts that this overwhelming nostalgia for a community defined in simplistic and trivial terms leads to an "unspecified feeling of loss and emptiness that in turn makes Americans vulnerable to the manipulation of symbols of community" (p. 144). Bender urges us to define community in terms of patterns of social interaction, not limiting it in time and space.

PROBLEMS IN DEFINING COMMUNITY

One of the persistent problems that arise for Bender (1978) and others is the role of locale in defining community. While geographic proximity has played an important role historically, communities are not necessarily neighborhoods today. Moreover, political efforts to enhance community through "local control" may be manipulative and self-serving to certain political actors. Bender warns us that "class intersects the notion of community and power; for the poor and the weak in our society, community seldom has any significant connections to the levers of power" (p. 149). This dilemma of the role of locale and community will prove to be one the most perplexing for schools.

Another dilemma in the definition of community is the importance of choice in our *gesellschaftlich* world, a concept foreign to a more traditional notion of community. We have become accustomed to a wide range of choices in the marketplace, and have begun to apply this to our personal lives. In *gemeinschaftlich* villages, since people could not opt out at any point, they came to some accommodation of their problems, even if the solution was not particularly desirable. We need to address the role of choice in communities today. Are we willing to give up some of our freedom to choose in order to develop more stable relationships?

Finally, can we meet our need for community in a world in which we have specialized relationships? Are diffuse relationships necessary for a community to function today? When we come together with a group of people with whom we share values and with whom we want to achieve some mutually desirable goal, will this relationship meet our need for a sense of belonging, or does it become another business endeavor, easily abandoned when the goal is no longer a priority for us?

Given that this conceptual system was developed during an era of urbanization and industrialization, it is understandable that the shift from *Gemeinschaft* to *Gesellschaft* came to be interpreted as inevitable. The continuum became simplistic and linear, predicting loss of *gemeinschaftlich* qualities of life, or said more directly, inevitable decline in community. However, this notion was challenged as anthropologists began studying cultures and how they changed in response to changing conditions. In the next chapter we will examine more contemporary reinterpretations of this line of community theory and look at questions of geographic proximity, choice, and specialized roles.

3

Modern Notions of Community

*The American dream is often a very private dream of being
the star, the uniquely successful and admirable one, the one
who stands out from the crowd of ordinary folk who don't
know how. And since we have believed in the dream for a
long time and worked very hard to make it come true, it is
hard for us to give it up, even though it contradicts another
dream we have—that of living in a society that would really
be worth living in.*

—*Bellah*, Habits of the Heart

We have seen that a number of writers have looked at ways *Gemeinschaft* reasserts itself into an apparently increasingly *Gesellschaft*
world. Redfield (1950, 1955) and Lewis (1951) looked at villages that
were adopting urban life-styles and noted that they retained many of
their folkways. Gans (1962) and Fischer (1982) looked at modern urban
and suburban groups and noted that they exhibited many folk characteristics. It appears that no matter how complex our world gets, the
need for human connectedness and belonging is strong, and people
have figured out ways to meet that need.

Even sociologists who formed many of our modern notions of bureaucracy found that the rules that defined the bureaucracy were often
compromised by individuals in personal ways. Parsons (1937) pointed
out that within the beaucracies of business, patterns of communication and loyalty often follow lines of cliques. He saw individuals in
bureaucracies as often being torn between individual friendships and
the norms of the institution.

Blau (1974), in his classic work on bureaucracy, agreed with the
position that Parsons (1937) took regarding the existence of personal
relationships within the bureaucratic workplace. He thought that Weber's (1925/1947) dichotomy between *Gemeinschaft* and *Gesellschaft*,
which was much like that of Tönnies (1887/1957), was too extreme. In
his study of work groups, he pointed out ways in which the informal

22

organization (*gemeinschaftlich* in nature) enabled *Gesellschaft* or formal organization to work.

A number of contemporary writers are dealing with issues of community today, recognizing that mobility, diversity, and choice are important factors. Some see ways in which community might be reestablished to take into account the complexity of life that seems inevitable in the late 20th century. As in the early communitarian movement, which saw how modern communication might link people in profound ways, some people today see technology as enabling community not bound by space. Still others see choice as an important feature of modern community, and one of the ways in which we can narrow the number of contacts we make in our lives in order to focus on a few important and intimate bonds. All of these writers wrestle with the problem of commitment and stability. If we are free to choose our associates at will, and we have a great number of options available, how can we build community that is stable and reliable, gives us a sense of belonging, and allows us to socialize our youth and order our lives?

These writers are not easy to categorize, as they have many common and overlapping themes. One group could be called loosely the modern communitarians, including such writers as Bellah (1985) and Etzioni (1993) and, more recently, Himmelfarb (1995) and Fukuyama (1995). They say that our survival and well-being depend on reinstituting some aspects of traditional community in modern life. A second group, which comes from a feminist tradition, includes Friedman (1982) and Young (1986), who say that traditional community is too restrictive and modern concepts must be broadened in certain ways. Yet another writer, Elshtain (1982, 1995), is a good example of the difficulty of categorizing in that she could fall into both groups. She comes from a feminist tradition and first wrote about the public and private aspects of women's lives, noting particularly the power of political action by women.

Writers may also be analyzed by the relationship they see between power and values. Some writers, the ones we have loosely categorized as communitarians, are primarily interested in reestablishing a strong set of morals and notions of virtue, and deal with community as the traditional vehicle for doing this. Others, including most of the feminists, come from a Marxist tradition and are interested in social organization and power. They see common values, morals, and virtues as deriving from the existing social organization and its power structure. Both groups wrestle with the problem of diversity in modern America and the difficulty of a common set of values. While these writers deal with schools only parenthetically, they examine community in light of late 20th century phenomena and may help us develop a more realistic concept of community as it pertains to schools.

MODERN COMMUNITARIANS

A number of writers have recently pointed out how segmented American society has become and in fact have asked if our country can continue to exist at any level of unification. These writers all advocate to some extent that a common belief system or code must unite all segments of our society if we are to continue. Himmelfarb (1994) and Etzioni (1993) chastise Americans for lack of a coherent system of morals. Schlesinger (1992), Sandel (1996), and Elshtain (1995) point out that the lack of a unifying civic belief system threatens the continuation of the United States as a democracy. All of these writers to some extent and for various reasons say that we have become overly concerned with the welfare of the individual at the expense of the welfare of society as a whole.

Several have turned their attention to Tocqueville's (1835/1945) keen insights into American character and society. Tocqueville, a Frenchman who traveled widely in 19th-century America, compared democracy here with democracy as it was emerging in Europe. He was particularly interested in the balance between a cohesive society and the individualism that he saw as such an important part of the American character, and he warned that the strong notion of individualism could eventually lead to isolation of individuals, threatening American democratic society. Tocqueville saw that Americans balanced individualism and society through family life, religious beliefs, and a unique tendency to form voluntary civic groups. He thought that this "art of association" (vol. 2, p. 118) not only gave hope to the isolating tendencies of the American character, but that it was through these groups that Americans were able to form a participatory democracy. Bellah (1985), Fukuyama (1995), and Putnam (1995) have all noted that Americans today are abandoning the voluntary organizations that characterized our society in the past. They see that these civic groups are the main vehicles Americans used for bridging the gap between the individual and society. Fukuyama suggests that this abandonment of voluntary associations is in large part responsible for the decline in social capital in America and leaves members of our society suspicious of others and overwhelmed by our individualism. A similar point is made by Putnam, who thinks that Americans' tendency to abandon voluntary associations in favor of isolating activities is a major desocializing force today.

Communities of Memory

Robert Bellah, in *Habits of the Heart* (1985), a term he takes from Tocqueville, explores the struggle in America between individualism and commitment to others. He suggests that balance between public and private aspects of life is key to the survival of modern society, and he studies the way these factors work in the lives of representative people. Bellah seems to find a unique combination of commitments among his subjects. For each, "the touchstones of truth and goodness lie in individual experience and intimate relations" (p. 250). He mentions several types of communities that meet this need in his subjects as he notes that "people develop loyalties to others in the context of families, small communities, religious congregations and life-style enclaves" (p. 250). He also found that people had a strong identification with the United States as a national community, and expected to be able to serve and connect in the public sphere.

One of the ways Bellah's (1985) subjects connected to the larger sphere was through civic organizations. As did Tocqueville (1835/1945), he notes the tendency of Americans to join groups of all kinds in order to achieve social or political ends. Bellah's theme of small, intermediate civic group's bridging the gap between the individual and the larger society will be picked up by other writers; we will note its relevance to schools.

Bellah (1985) noted several problems in the way his subjects related to others that are exacerbated by the mobility and diversity of modern life. The public connection appeared to be fragile and to fall victim to frustration and burnout when people moved or the local scene changed. He suggested that Americans have a fear of not being able to relate to people who are too different, which leads to the "tremendous nostalgia many Americans have for the small town" (p. 251).

Bellah (1985) offers a definition of community. He speaks of "real communities" as "communities of memory," which are "constituted by their past" (p. 153). In telling the stories of a community, members develop coherence and identity. He notes the difficulty of neighborhoods or locations' being communities of memory because of Americans' geographic mobility. Yet "without history and hope, community means only the gathering of the similar" (p. 154), what he calls life-style enclaves. He says the longing for the idealized small town is really a longing for meaning and coherence. He points out the emptiness of unfettered individualism and suggests that it leads to a culture of separation, as feared by Tocqueville (1835/1945). Like Elshtain (1995) and Schleshinger (1992), Bellah calls for a new culture of coherence, in which we think about the traditions that give meaning to our lives, as in our communities of memory. He thinks that only this way can we restore America's belief in democracy and the political system.

Moral Commitment and Responsibility

The strongest communitarian voice in modern America is that of Amitai Etzioni (1993), one of the founders of the modern communitarian movement. He speaks in passionate terms of bringing about moral reconstruction based on family and on schools that teach a moral tradition. Etzioni decries a modern America in which people are too concerned with rights at the expense of responsibilities. He makes specific recommendations concerning schools—that morals be taught explicitly, that students be required to perform public service, and that schools be set up in such a way as to promote bonding between student and teacher, perhaps having longer and fewer instructional periods each day in high school, or making each high school teacher teach several subjects to the same group of students.

Etzioni (1993) mentions Tönnies's conceptual framework of *Gemeinschaft* and *Gesellschaft* (1887/1957) taking the common, but too narrow, view that writers of that era all saw *Gemeinschaft* as primitive and repressive. While recognizing that traditional small-town *Gemeinschaft* cannot be reconstructed today, Etzioni attempts to show communities that can take into account the nature of modern life by recognizing nongeographic communities, such as work communities. He also recognizes that traditional communities were homogeneous and that new communities have to find a way to accommodate diversity. He suggests that communities today must begin at the level of the family and be reinforced at increasingly broad levels like "Chinese nesting boxes" (p. 32). In this way smaller homogeneous subcommunities group themselves into a larger social web. He feels that these communities can all agree on a basic set of morals while varying in other ways. Calling for a "new *Gemeinschaft* that would be neither repressive nor hierarchical" (p. 122), he sees American society accommodating diverse subcommunities by being a kind of "supracommunity—a community of communities" (p. 160).

Etzioni (1993) assumes that most Americans share a unifying set of core values and fails to deal with how to reconcile deeply held differences. He ultimately leaves his readers to decide which are the shared values and which are the separate identifying values. The values that are generally shared are often vague; it is values of the second type, unique to a smaller group, that are more typical of real communities and that lead to greater separation.

Etzioni (1993) is really pleading for a strengthening of the moral commitment of Americans, and uses the term *community* as a vehicle. In his movement, people sign on to a manifesto of principles regarding responsibility to others. This differs to a great extent from traditional *Gemeinschaft*, because the bond in traditional *Gemeinschaft* was a naturally occurring phenomenon between people who were linked by kinship, ethnicity, geography, and so forth. It was not a matter of choice—no manifesto was necessary. Etzioni attempts to make a case that people should feel a commitment to others, namely American society at large, and this is problematic. People do not feel natural bonds to anonymous "others"—especially people as different from each other as those in American society today. To create such a bond, Etzioni argues, is in people's best interest, but this commitment begins to take on the contractual nature of *Gesellschaft*. It is really like the code of behavior that comes from such legal sources as the Constitution. Etzioni could make his case equally well by simply stressing that legal structures today have become too concerned with rights at the expense of responsibilities, and could advocate remedies by restructuring laws.

CRITICAL VIEWS: PROBLEMS OF POWER AND DIFFERENCE

Criticism of reestablishing *Gemeinschaft* often comes from those groups of people who were constrained in traditional communities. The strong sense of identity in *Gemeinschaft* often came at the cost of excluding others—a sense of "our people" involved identifying a group of people who are not "like us." Stability of role definition within a *Gemeinschaft* also led people who were in subordinate roles, or roles that they perceived as subordinate, to object to traditional community. The goals of justice and equality in America inevitably come into conflict with the exclusionary aspect of *Gemeinschaft*. This can be handled in several ways, but each has its problems. Different communities of equal standing can exist, but as we have seen over and over, power is not equally distributed, and communities differ widely in their power and wealth. The community can be defined so broadly as to include everyone, thus losing the identity function of community, or it can be seen as Etzioni's idea of subcommunities within a supracommunity—the Chinese nesting boxes—with congruent value systems.

Feminist writers have also been interested in community and the "socially defined self." They share the communitarians' concern that the theme of individualism has become too dominant in today's world, perhaps to the point of destroying our social connections. On the other hand, they are concerned that modern communitarians' focus on family and neighborhood will be restrictive to women. We will examine two feminists writers as examples of people who see the value in the connectedness of community but object to the exclusionary nature or restrictive nature of traditional roles.

Communities of Choice

Based on the work of Gilligan (1982), Marilyn Friedman (1982) suggests that women seek connections with others as an end in itself, while men affiliate in order to accomplish some other end. This theme bears a striking resemblance to Tönnies' (1887/1957) original conception of *Gemeinschaft* as feminine and *Gesellschaft* as masculine. In fact, Friedman criticizes the communitarians for "providing no basis for regarding the nurturant, relational self as morally superior to those who are highly individualistic" (p. 148). She further questions communitarians in their call for communities to make moral claims on their members, without any apparent ability to avoid practices that might be exclusionary or suppressive. Finally, she questions the communitarian notion that community is a connection one discovers rather than chooses.

Friedman (1982) notes that today people are involved simultaneously in a number of communities, and suggests a model for "communities of choice" patterned after women's friendships and urban social networks. She suggests that they are a better model for community in that friendships are voluntary, express deep commitment from the social self, and can accommodate the multiplicity of relationships required by modern urban living. Friedman admits that these communities often have no common history, such as described by Bellah's (1985) "community of memory," and she recognizes that children and elderly people cannot depend on a community in which members are free to leave at will. Thus Friedman deals successfully with the issues of choice and diversity, but fails to address the issue of stability. Communities of choice are always vulnerable to members' moving or choosing to emphasize different interests or aspects of their identity, and forming new patterns of association. While she gives examples of voluntary

associations that serve to define the self, these are often associations
of people who feel excluded from society in general, such as ethnic
groups or lesbian groups. She has no real mechanism otherwise for
differentiating a community that meets a deep-seated need for belonging from an affinity group that is merely formed for recreation or con-
venience.

Communities and Otherness

Iris Marion Young (1986) deals explicitly with the deep, identity giving
nature of community. She suggests that much of the identity of community comes from excluding certain others, and that community by
most communitarian standards requires an understanding and shared
subjectivity among members such that the boundary between community members disappears. This is possible only with people who are
very much alike, and this defining quality makes community among
people who are very different quite impossible. She further questions
the requirement that community be based on face-to-face or unmedi-
ated relations. She feels that such ideas of community are "both wildly
utopian and undesirable" (p. 18). Ultimately, she abandons the word
community with these aforementioned connotations and meanings
and calls for "social relationships that embody openness to unassimilated otherness with justice and appreciation" (p. 23). Young, like Friedman (1982), sees a model for modern relationships in the complexity
of urban life. In a city, strangers share space for commercial, social, or
aesthetic purposes; people experience the ethnicity or customs of others without adopting them as their own. Thus in describing the ways
groups might coexist to gain certain benefits, Young echoes much
original social contract theory and may have brought us full circle in
differentiating between *Gemeinschaft* and *Gesellschaft*. Indeed, her
"social relationships of unassimilated otherness," in which groups interact for mutual advantage, is essentially *Gesellschaft*, as defined by
Tönnies (1887/1957).

THE ROLE OF CIVIC LIFE

Several modern writers have dealt explicitly with the lack of a unifying
civic belief system in America today. While Etzioni (1993) assumed
that Americans are unified at some very basic level, other writers say
that we find more identity in the belief systems that divide us than
in those that unite us. In addressing these conflicting loyalties and

identities, Elshtain (1995) and Schlesinger (1992) call us to develop a new, unifying covenant, and Sandel (1996) asks that we learn to live with the ambiguity of multiple and conflicting levels of loyalty.

Advocates of a New Covenant

In his *Disuniting of America*, Arthur Schlesinger (1992) states that the lack of a unifying American identity is "the culmination of the cult of ethnicity" (p. 119). He sees that America has always struggled with the differences of ethnic groups and that recently groups have misstated history and misused the schools in an attempt to secure their own identity at the expense of that of the nation. While he urges us to a better balance of *pluribus* and *unum* and scolds ethnic groups for these self-centered actions, he gives little guidance in how we might handle the problems of difference and power.

Jean Bethke Elshtain (1982, 1995), who also advocates a new covenant, deals explicitly with the problems of difference and power, as she explores the relationship of public and private lives, specifically along gender lines. In *Daughters of Antigone* she looked at the question of conflicting loyalties to family and to the state, which she originally casts as a conflict for women, but could as easily be seen as a *Gemeinschaft/Gesellschaft* conflict. In her more recent book, *Democracy on Trial*, she calls explicitly for a new social covenant to restore the civil society that seems to be disintegrating today. Elshtain points out, as do Fukuyama (1995) and Putnam (1995), that Americans now seem unable or unwilling to form the civic and social associations that Tocqueville (1835/1945) said were necessary to maintain our form of democracy. Fukuyama describes these institutions as the bridge between the family and larger society. Elshtain (1995) calls these "mediating institutions" between the individual and the state; she describes how traditionally a child was nested in a family, and the family in turn was

> nested within a wider, overlapping framework of sustaining and supporting civic institutions: churches, schools and solidaristic associations such as unions or mothers' associations. American society was honeycombed by a vast network that offered a densely textured social ecology for the growing citizen. (pp. 5–6)

Elshtain concludes that, despite American's traditionally antistate tendency, today we find ourselves asking the state to hold us together in the absence of these organizations.

Ambiguity of Multiple Identities

Sandel (1996) also considers the role of the state in giving identity to the individual and coherence to a community. He differs from Elshtain (1995) in his conclusion that the "nation-state," historically identified by a small, bounded geographic area, can no longer function in this role. Sandel traces the history of political power in America as an example of how nation-states today are pressured internally and externally. Global economics and trade have important consequences everywhere, and no longer is a people's well-being determined only by their own laws and industry. Throughout the world nation-states are also threatened internally by smaller ethnic, geographic, or religious subgroups seeking individual identity and sovereignty. Sandel concludes that today we cannot look to our nation-state as the unifying ideal that gives us security, identity, and a sense of well-being. We must recognize that simultaneously we are citizens of the world, a nation-state, various regional entities, and a multiplicity of ethnic, religious, or affinity groups. For Sandel "the civic virtue distinctive in our time is the capacity to negotiate our way through sometimes overlapping and conflicting obligations that lay claim to us and live with the tension to which multiple loyalties give rise" (p. 74). Thus Sandel suggests that people must adapt to the nature of the world today rather than trying to redirect the course of society to the way people have been.

Sandel (1996) suggests that "such politics demands citizens who can abide the ambiguity associated with divided sovereignty, who can think and act as multiply situated selves" (p. 74). In these suggestions, perhaps more than anywhere, we begin to see an answer consistent with the *Gemeinshaft/Gesellschaft* analysis. In fact, we belong to groups that are at various places on the continuum, and each group to which we belong may have characteristics from several places on the continuum at the same time.

CONCLUSION

This discussion brings us to a point where we see that there are several things missing in our lives today because of loss of community in the traditional, *gemeinschaftlich* sense. Among these are lacks in a sense of belonging, social monitoring, traditional socialization of youth, and the ability to take care of people's needs in an immediate way.

There are several other aspects of modern life that may preclude, or might be precluded by, traditional community. Among these are geographic mobility, role specialization, choice, and the notion of equality of individuals. These are aspects of our lives that are generally valued and that we might not be willing to give up.

Traditionally there have been intermediate organizations in America that bridged the gap between family and society. But schools may be one of the last vestiges of such organizations as we tend to turn over more and more of our social and civic responsibility to the state or to large bureaucratic organizations. In fact, Drucker (1994) posits that social service organizations will become a third large sector similar to the private and public sectors. He predicts that this social sector, made up of large hospitals, nonprofit organizations, mega-churches, and so forth, will do the work that has traditionally been done by the community.

With such changes in intermediate organizations, we must ask a series of questions about schools:

- What roles do schools play in this time of changing social expectations?
- Do schools alone bear responsibility for socializing the individual into the larger society?
- Are schools expected to give a sense of self-identity and belonging?
- Are schools alone the vehicle by which children learn the ways they are similar to and different from others?

We turn now to an examination of schools and community and look at some of these issues.

4

Drifting Toward *Gesellschaft*:
The Schools' Identity Crisis

Though most principals, superintendents, and teachers have a
desire to do better and are working as hard as they can to pro-
vide a quality education to every student they serve, the road
is rough and the going is slow. The lead villain in this frustrat-
ing drama is the loss of community in our schools and in soci-
ety itself.
— *Sergiovanni*, Building Community in Schools

Sergiovanni's (1994) words capture the central focus of this book—the "community movement" in education and the urgency of the arguments surrounding it. Indeed, Sergiovanni and others see the "loss of community" as the heart of the problem of educational reform and the building of community as a sort of panacea for educational ills. Others may disagree, and not all reforms are concerned with community. However, many reforms do indeed address the community issue, as we discussed in Chapter 1. "Community-connection experiments" (Crowson & Boyd, 1993), such as parent-involvement programs and site-based management, attempt to strengthen the links between schools and local communities, while community-building efforts attempt to reconstitute the school itself as more community-like (Bryk, 1988; McLaughlin & Talbert, 1990; Reyes, 1994; Sergiovanni, 1994).

In the first three chapters, we briefly reviewed the community movement in education and the theoretical frames we are using to examine it, and discussed some contemporary notions of community. In Chapters 5 and 6, we explore the promise of reforms focusing on schools and community. First, however, we believe it is important to analyze and understand the conditions being addressed by these reforms. In this chapter, then, we look more closely at the source of the community issue in schools. *Why* do schools lack "community," and why are they out of touch with the local communities they serve? We will use the *Gemeinschaft/Gesellschaft* framework as an analytical tool to address these questions. In this discussion, we are presenting our own analysis based on application of this theoretical framework. In some ways, our views are similar to those of Sergiovanni (1994), who refers often to the *Gemeinschaft/Gesellschaft* framework in his call for community building in schools. However, we depart from Sergiovanni in looking more closely at the institutional and social forces that have created the community "crisis" and draw different conclusions about the prospects for community in education. Our argument is that the schools have drifted significantly to *Gesellschaft*, and that this drift is damaging to both connections with local community and the sense of community within the school. The drift toward *Gesellschaft* is mostly unintentional and is certainly not a "plot" on the part of any segment of society (e.g., "corporate America") to take over the schools. Rather, we think it is a product of several long-term societal and educational trends. In the next sections, we discuss our analysis of these trends, using the lens of the *Gemeinschaft/Gesellschaft* framework. Then we summarize how the drift toward *Gesellschaft* has affected community issues in schools, as background for considering the promise of reforms.

THE *GEMEINSCHAFT/GESELLSCHAFT* "MIX" IN ORGANIZATIONS

Institutions and organizations, like individuals, exist in a bifurcated social world in which the values of *Gemeinschaft* and *Gesellschaft* interact. The relative *salience*, however, of *Gemeinschaft* and *Gesellschaft* within the organization has a major impact on relationships within the organization and on the organization's relationship to its environment. If we think of the *Gemeinschaft/Gesellschaft* distinction as a continuum, where a particular organization sits on the continuum depends partly on its purpose. A private, for-profit business, for example, has the central purpose of generating profits for owners and shareholders, and this purpose translates into several other goals — containing the costs of production, conducting effective marketing campaigns, and so forth. The values of the marketplace prevail in the profit-oriented business; relationships are contractual, and the "rational will" of *Gesellschaft* dominates. As Tönnies (1887/1957) observed, "the natural content of such an order [the corporation] can be comprised in the one formula: *'Pacta esse observanda'* — contracts must be executed" (p. 75). Economic pressures of the marketplace force the business to make "tough" (rational-will) decisions. If profits are down and production costs up, then workers must be laid off. It is common knowledge that Western profit-making corporations are becoming ever more ruthless in application of these operating principles—"job security" is becoming an anachronism (Bridges, 1994). It follows, then, that the quality of relationships within the *Gesellschaft*-dominated business world lack the trust and loyalty of *Gemeinschaft*. Relationships tend to be formal and distant, shaped by coporate role expectations.

Moving along the continuum, government and nonprofit agencies, though not driven by the marketplace, tend to be dominated by *Gesellschaft* as well. A city police force, for example, has the limited purpose of maintaining law and order, or, more narrowly, protecting citizens from crime. The performance of the police force is governed by contractual arrangements with the citizenry and a variety of legal constraints. In our current society, a police officer typically does not know the persons he or she is protecting or arresting; the officer does the job according to the legal contract because he or she is paid to do it. Similarly, social service agencies such as public health departments operate by "contract" with the citizenry to provide services. Public health case workers are paid to serve their clients. In both these examples, individual workers (the policeperson, the social worker) may have altruistic motives to "help" others, which resemble the "natural will" of *Gemeinschaft*. But the actual performance of their duties, and their roles in their organizations, are governed by contract. These organizations, then, do not represent Tönnies' (1887/1957) communities of place, kinship, or mind.

In contrast, most churches are closer to the *Gemeinschaft* pole of the continuum. The typical mainstream church in American society is a "gathered community" of individuals who voluntarily associate because of shared spiritual values. In Tönnies' (1887/1957) terms, churches are examples of communities of mind, in the sense that spiritual interests are an aspect of mind. Church members gather together for the primary purpose of *being together* because they share spiritual values, not to fulfill contractual agreements regarding their obligations to each other or to society. At the same time, the organizational aspects of churches may be quite *gesellschaftlich*. Management staff may be hired under a contractual arrangement, and church members may be expected to pledge an amount of money to support church functions. The point of these examples (police force, social service agency, and church) is that all organizations are a mix of *Gesellschaft* and *Gemeinschaft*. Even within the market-driven, for-profit business, a "community" of sorts, based in friendship, may exist among groups of workers. But the relative *dominance* of *Gemeinschaft* or *Gesellschaft* will differ, sometimes dramatically, from organization to organization, and may shift over time. In Bender's (1978) words, the analytical interest becomes the "interaction and interplay of communal and noncommunal ways in the lives of all" (p. 43) and the relative importance of the quality at either end of the continuum.

Schools, like the other organizational examples, present a mix of *Gemeinschaft* and *Gesellschaft* qualities. Public schools are first and foremost government agencies. They exist through contractual agreements with the citizenry for a specific purpose—to "educate" the children of the local community. They are not voluntary "gathered communities" of mind in the same sense as churches. Citizens' participation in the service provided by public schools is not always voluntary—children's attendance is legally mandated—and staff participation is primarily due to contractual agreements. It is probably valid to say that educators—teachers and administrators—gather together in schools not so much around shared values as from the need to make a living. Working conditions, expectations, and formal relationships among faculty and between faculty and administrators are governed to a large extent by the "contract" and by institutional expectations of performance, not by the "natural will" of *Gemeinschaft*.

On the other hand, schools have some strong *Gemeinschaft* qualities. Educators are involved in one of the most intimate "community" functions, the care and nurturance of children. Further, it is both common wisdom and empirically established that teachers are primarily motivated by the intrinsic satisfaction of working with and helping children. And within schools, as in other organizations, true gathered communities based on common values and friendship exist informally among staff and students. Given this mix of characteristics, a central analytical question in looking at schools is how and why the relative salience of *Gemeinschaft* and *Gesellschaft* has changed over the years, and how this shift has affected the school's role as a community and in relation to the local community it serves.

GEMEINSCHAFT ROOTS OF SCHOOLS:
THE WAY WE WERE

In its earliest forms, the public school was deeply connected to the traditional local community that it served. This local community was fairly homogeneous and stable, marked by close kinship ties and shared values. The school and its course of study were an extension of the homes, the church, and the commerce of the community; the boundaries between the school and the community were indistinct. Tyack (1974) says of these "village schools": "School and community were organically related in a tightly knit group in which people met face to face and knew each other's affairs" (p. 17).

Gradually, the public school evolved to serve as a "bridge" between two social worlds, *Gemeinschaft* and *Gesellschaft*. As cities and commerce expanded, the expectations for the bridging function of education increased. The school served as a valued link to *Gesellschaft* by educating children in the ways of the wider American society—the ways of competitive commerce and participatory democracy beyond the local community. The school provided children with the skills of communication and commerce needed for social and economic success. But while the school was to provide tools for life outside the local community, it remained the first social system beyond the family and church; as such, it was expected to support local values and mores. Thus, in the earliest years of public schooling, "local control" referred not only to political governance arrangements, but also to the community's sense of ownership, or "moral" control, of the school's program. Tyack (1974) states that "most rural patrons had little doubt that the school was theirs to control . . . and not the property of the professional educator" (p. 17). Similarly, Tyack describes the "harmonious relationship" (p. 103) that existed between schools in urban areas and the relatively homogeneous neighborhoods they served.

Historically, then, the American public school developed a balance between *Gemeinschaft* and *Gesellschaft*. While a tension between these roles no doubt existed, a workable balance was the norm. The local community supported the "bridge" function of the school. They believed the school was a necessary supplement to the family and that education was the key to success in the larger society. More important, the local community supported the values of *Gesellschaft*— the ideals of democracy, individualism, free enterprise, and economic opportunity that supposedly prevailed in the larger society. Immigrant groups in the cities, particularly, "saw schooling as a doorway to new opportunities" (Tyack, 1974, p. 241). Thus, in earlier years, local community members felt a sense of ownership of the school, valued its role as a bridge to *Gesellschaft*, and trusted its efficacy in fulfilling this role.

FORCES OF CHANGE – DRIFTING
TOWARD *GESELLSCHAFT*

Throughout the 20th century, several trends have eroded this workable balance between *Gemeinschaft* and *Gesellschaft* in the schools. The schools have drifted far closer to the *Gesellschaft* pole, and this drift has affected both the quality of life in schools and the relationship between schools and the communities they serve. In this section, we examine three of these forces of change.

The Corporate Model and Political Reform

Throughout this century, schools as organizations have become more bureaucratic and governance of schools has become more centralized. Raymond Callahan (1962), David Tyack, and Elizabeth Hansot (Tyack, 1974; Tyack & Hansot, 1982) have written critical histories of American education that clearly document the origins of the corporate, bureaucratic model for school organization and the gradual shift to state-level centralized governance. Tyack (1974), in particular, traces the "success story" of the administrative progressives, who joined forces with business leaders and university professors to bring organizational change and political reform to public schools. The administrative progressives admired the efficiency of corporate structures and the use of "scientific" methods for classifying and organizing students. Their success in importing these ideas into schools resulted in an explosion of the superstructure of schools and a proliferation of specialized roles, with an "expert" superintendent at the top of the hierarchy.

The progressives' political reform agenda contributed to bureaucratization and the erosion of local control. As Tyack (1974) explains, under the guise of "keeping the schools out of politics" (p. 132), the progressives pushed for smaller, nonpartisan, districtwide school boards with members elected at large, rather than from neighborhood wards. This shift in method of selection favored the upper-middle and upper classes, who had the time and financial resources to run for public office. Reform led to election of a few "successful men" to local boards. These persons represented the elite class of business and professionals rather than the largely working classes who were served by neighborhood schools. Tyack (1974) states:

> As men who had perfected large organizations, they had national reference groups and thought in cosmopolitan rather than merely local terms. Suc-

cessful in their own careers, they assumed that what was good for their class and private institutions was good public policy as well. (p. 130)

Thus, through political reform, both the corporate, bureaucratic model for school organization and the values of the elite leaders of business came to dominate the schools.

The long-term effects of bureaucratization, centralization, and political reform have been to weaken ties between the school and local community and to make the school itself less community-like. Though a "local" school board supposedly represented school-district citizens, the local community around a neighborhood school was essentially disenfranchised, at least in larger districts. The community around the neighborhood school lost its sense of ownership of the school's program, which was now driven by the preferences of the business elites on the central school board. The school became a collection of professionals serving the student "clients," rather than an extension of the community. In terms of the *Gemeinschaft/Gesellschaft* continuum, the school shifted away from its close ties to *Gemeinschaft* values. The values of *Gesellschaft*—the corporate world and the marketplace—came to dominate schools. For parents in the local neighborhood community, then, the school would no longer look like a safe, community-controlled "bridge" to success in the *gesellschaftlich* world for their children. Rather, it would appear to be an intimidating institution run by professionals, in the service of the economic interests of the elites. It follows that continued parental trust in the schools would hinge on trust in the values of *Gesellschaft*, a point to which we will return later.

A second effect of bureaucratization and centralization was to change relationships *within* schools so that schools became less community-like. The corporate model and centralized control by "experts" led to a proliferation of rules and regulations to govern the work lives of educators. The hierarchy of the corporate model suggests a line of authority and control in which expert administrators supervise and direct subordinate teachers. And the idea of education as "science" has led increasingly to a view of teachers as technicians carrying out orders and fulfilling the prescriptions of the experts. Educators' roles have become "contractualized," especially through negotiated union contracts. Further the business values imported into education have created a mind set of educational "productivity," with student learning as units of production. The outcome is that relationships within schools increasingly emulate the corporate world governed by "rational will," rather than the "natural will" of caring for children.

Neighborhood/Community Change

The second trend shifts our focus to the local community surrounding the school. The nature of this local community has indeed changed, and these changes are often considered indicators of community decline. Changes in families have been well documented (Coleman, 1987; Hoffer & Coleman, 1990). Communities of kinship are practically nonexistent in our mobile society, as extended families live in scattered locations. Relationships among families within a neighborhood have changed in a number of ways. People work farther from their homes and tend not to encounter their neighbors during the course of a work day. The number of face-to-face contacts with neighbors has decreased dramatically. Interchangeable suburbs have replaced most identifiable neighborhoods, and some traditionally ethnic neighborhoods have disappeared (Coleman, 1985; Wagstaff & Gallagher, 1990).

Although *Gemeinschaft* may "persist" as an essential human need (Bender, 1978), it is in a more fragmented form. In fact, it may be that the only forms of *Gemeinschaft* to persist in modern society are the vestiges of community of kinship found in nuclear families, gathered community of mind as represented in churches, and "lifestyle enclaves" (Bellah, 1985, p. 250) as discussed in Chapter 3, and some urban ethnic enclaves. Communities of place and extended communities of kinship, as defined by Tönnies (1887/1957), are practically extinct. Thus, the local community served by the neighborhood school is no longer a "community" in the *Gemeinschaft* sense, but rather a collection of small family units that may or may not live in a life-style enclave and participate in other gathered communities. Lacking shared values and kinship ties, the local community lacks a coherent voice to influence the school. The local community has few weapons with which to combat the disenfranchisement created by political reform and the legacy of the "administrative progressives."

Erosion of Trust in Democratic Ideals

The third trend contributing to the shift toward *Gesellschaft* in schools is the gradual erosion of public trust in our nation's democratic ideals and its public institutions. There seems to be little consensus in the late 20th century around national goals or a national ethic. Instead, the values of the corporate world—profit and competition—have come to dominate the larger society, to crowd out the traditional ideals of democratic participation, individualism, and free-enterprise opportunity. We tend to be disillusioned with our political and institutional leaders, who are no longer able to provide the symbolic leadership needed for a democracy. Slater, Bolman, Crow, Goldring, and Thurston (1994) state:

> Democracies carry with them a strong tendency toward crises of meaning, that is, alienation. One of the chief correctives for this tendency is a new kind of leadership that is capable of a restoration and revitalization of the . . . symbolic system. . . . A chief function of leadership in a democracy, therefore, is symbolic; it is to help restore the meaning and common purpose to daily life that was lost in the transition from community to society. And, for this reason, leadership is always of high interest in a democracy. (p. 28).

Our national leaders have failed to provide this symbolic leadership around inspirational democratic ideals. The national society is dominated by the values of the marketplace. Disillusionment with these values is particularly acute for persons in poverty and for persons whose access to the economic mainstream is impeded by cultural and language barriers.

This erosion of public trust has important implications both for school-community connections and for the sense of community within the school. First, as we stated earlier, the school is no longer firmly linked to *gemeinschaftlich* values of the local community. Instead, due to longitudinal developments in school governance and culture, the school has come to symbolize *gesellschaftlich* values of the corporate world: efficiency and productivity. The perceived mission of the schools has gradually shifted to serving the economic interests of the elites, who control the school's governance, rather than the interests of the local community. Parental trust in the school therefore hinges on respect for and trust in these values. As the trust in national democratic values has eroded, so has the trust in the school's mission.

Where the school once represented hallowed American ideals of individual opportunity balanced with the responsibilities of democratic citizenship and was viewed as a useful "bridge" to success in the larger society, it now represents the morally impoverished values of *Gesellschaft*. Since many people no longer aspire to participate successfully in this *Gesellschaft*, many people no longer trust or find meaning in the school's mission (Tyack & Hansot, 1982). Wagstaff and Gallagher (1990) state:

> It is a long-recognized bond between schools and parents to turn children into productive citizens. Yet many American families in the 1980s are

either unable or unwilling to shape, support, stimulate, or encourage their children in the traditional ways schools expect. (p. 94)

Educators frequently interpret this alienation from the school's expectations as a failure on the part of families and communities, a symptom of dysfunctionality, without realizing that the *school's* values and sense of mission may be dysfunctional, that the school is experiencing an identity crisis in terms of its purpose. This identity crisis contributes to weakened links between school and community.

Second, this erosion of public trust affects educators as well, their sense of purpose and mission in schools, and therefore their sense of community. What are schools for? What is our "mission" as educators? Is it, as *Gesellschaft* values would have it, to prepare "Workforce 2000" to ensure national economic competitiveness? It is hard to find inspiration in this *Gesellschaft* vision for schooling. Educators are left without a compelling, shared vision for their work. And without a shared sense of purpose, we lack a sense of community within our schools.

Summary

We argue that American public schools have shifted dramatically from *Gemeinschaft* to *Gesellschaft* during the 20th century. There is no one cause for or culprit in this shift; rather, the interplay of a number of trends has pushed the schools to the *gesellschaftlich* pole of the continuum. Bureaucratization, centralization, and political reform have created a new *gesellschaftlich* culture in schools, one dominated by the values of the marketplace and estranged from local community values and control. As Bryk (1988) states, "Schools are preparing students for a competitive, individualistic, secular, and materialistic world" (p. 260). Relationships within schools have become "contractualized" and dominated by the "rational will" of *Gesellschaft*. To a great extent, we have lost in schools the qualities and experiences associated with the "natural will" of *Gemeinschaft*: trust, belongingness, security, and permanence. A strong *prima facie* case can be made that the loss of these qualities is a serious problem for schools, resulting in alienation of students, parents, and educators. Changes in the local community have resulted in fragmentation of communities of place and kinship, so that the local community lacks a coherent "voice" to influence the school. And the erosion of national democratic ideals has left the school bereft of an inspirational mission that would maintain parental trust in the school and provide a rallying "vision" for educators' work. As Johnson (1990) puts it, public schools seem characterized by "mixed purposes, hazy histories, artificial traditions, and a neutral stance toward values" (p. 220). Overall, the dramatic shift toward *Gesellschaft* in schools alienates the vestiges of local community from the school and reduces the sense of community within schools. The school is in the midst of an identity crisis regarding whose interests it serves and what it stands for.

THE COMMUNITY ISSUE AND REFORM

This analysis surfaces a number of intriguing and troubling issues. For one, if the school's identity crisis is one of the major causes of alienation from community, then the question that follows is whether the school can shape a new identity, a new sense of mission, that will regain the trust and commitment of the local community and be inspirational to educators. Is it *possible* for educators to shape this new identity and mission, given the current organizational and political contexts for schooling? Might this mission be to educate children for participation in a *multicultural democracy*? In so doing, could schools be instrumental in regeneration of a national civic morality based in democratic ideals? Some interesting work is emerging around these questions. Radical humanist critics of education have for some time called for a new mission for schools, one consonant with the ideals of a "multicultural/multiracial democracy." Greene (1993), Giroux (1992a, 1992b), Lomotey (1990), and McLaren (1993) represent this perspective in their work. Lomotey (1990), in summarizing this perspective, writes that schools should

> prefigure the larger society that we want. Their programs should prepare students to transverse many worlds, acquiring fluency in many cultural codes, including those of the historically oppressed and those of the historically powerful political and economic oppressors. (pp. 4–5)

In a similar vein, Giroux (1992b) argues:

> The most important task facing educators is not about collecting data or managing competencies, but constructing a pedagogical and political vision which recognizes that the problems with American schools lie in the realm of values, ethics, and vision. Put another way, educating for democracy begins not with test scores but with the questions: What kinds of citizens do we hope to produce through public education? What kind of society do we want to create? This involves educating students to live in a critical democracy. (p. 11)

Though emerging from a different theoretical perspective, postmodern curriculum theorists pose a similar argument—that schools should reflect the complexity and multiple narratives of postmodern life to help students function in such a world (Slattery, 1995).

While the radical humanists and the postmodern theorists offer moving arguments and a glimmer of hope for creating a new sense of mission for schools, which are worthy of further analysis and exploration, their ideas are not often translated into concrete reform efforts. Their discourse proceeds in the scholarly literature and is often "suspect" to practitioners because of its theoretical links to neo-Marxism, social reproduction, and critical theory. In this book, we wish to focus on reforms that *are* being implemented and ideas that are more accessible to practitioners than those of the critical humanists. Some of these ideas are being implemented through state-mandated reform initiatives (e.g., school-based management), while others are implemented through local projects.

For our purposes, we group these reforms into two types: (1) "community-connections experiments" (Crowson & Boyd, 1993), which are aimed at shoring up links between school and local community (included here are school-based/shared-decision-making models, collaborations between schools and other community agencies, and parent-involvement programs); and (2) community-building efforts within schools, aimed at making the school culture more community-like (e.g., Sergiovanni, 1994). In the following two chapters, we look more closely at some of these reforms and their promise for community building. In evaluating their promise, we must consider the underlying trends that have created the community issue in schools, and whether the reforms address these trends. In addition, we must consider whether the reforms are realistic in terms of the possibilities for community that exist in our modern world and the need for a *Gemeinschaft/Gesellschaft* balance in schools. The application of reform "Band-Aids" to the community issue that does not get at the deeper issues we have identified in this chapter is unlikely to create much change, in our view.

CONCLUSION

The school-community issue is embedded in a complex interplay of social forces. The two sides of the community issue—school-community connections and school as community—interact and are both related to larger societal problems of democratic ideals and leadership.

Superficial efforts to create community in schools are not likely to have much impact unless the larger picture is considered. We may work hard in individual schools and districts, for example, to create a "vision" for schooling to serve as the basis for community building. But if the *Gesellschaft* philosophy of education and values of the marketplace that dominate national education policy and local school practice remain unquestioned and unchallenged, the problem remains the same—we are left with "mixed purposes" and "artificial traditions" (Johnson, 1990). What, then, is the promise of community-focused reforms? We turn to this question in the next chapter.

5

The Promise of Reform: Rebuilding School-Community Connections

Teachers and principals ought to find ways to share with parents their convictions and to win them over — or allow parents to change the direction of the school . . . to be responsive to the wisdom that arises from a consensus of parents' groups. . . . Schools need to involve parents much more, both in order for the schools to be able to discharge their duties (which requires active parental backing) and because empowering parents is a way of building community.
— *Etzioni*, The Spirit of Community

Educators are bombarded with calls for reform by politicians at the national and state levels, by parent groups, by religious groups, and by many other stakeholders in education. These reforms often conflict because they spring from fundamentally different core values for education and from conflicting views of teaching and learning. While debates continue as to the value of many of these initiatives, particularly whether they have any effect on instructional *practice* (Cuban, 1990; Elmore, 1996; Sarason, 1990), the reform trend continues into the late 1990s. In this chapter, we will apply the *Gemeinschaft/Gesellschaft* framework to an analysis of the current reform movement and begin to examine reforms aimed at school-community connections.[1]

CHARACTERIZING SCHOOL REFORMS

Typically, the contemporary reform movement is visualized in "waves." "First-wave" reforms grew out of a concern with American

---

1. In this chapter, and particularly in the section on coordination of services to children, we draw from our earlier analysis of the reform movement (Furman & Merz, 1996).

economic competitiveness and were launched by the national reports of the early 1980s, particularly *A Nation at Risk* (National Commission on Excellence in Education, 1983). These reforms focused on higher standards for both students and teachers along with greater standardization of the curriculum and assessments. Typical first-wave reforms were higher graduation requirements, competency testing for students, and teacher testing for certification (Fuhrman, Elmore, & Massell, 1993).The "second wave" soon followed, as a sort of backlash against the first. Where the first wave attempted to standardize and control teaching through centralized regulations, the second wave focused on teacher professionalism and decentralized decision making (Bacharach, 1990). Examples of second-wave reforms would be teacher teaming, school-based management, and parental-choice initiatives. Even a "third wave" is seen in so-called systemic reforms, which aim for comprehensive, simultaneous change in many aspects of the education system (Jacobson & Berne, 1993).

As an alternative to the "wave" metaphor, we offer the *Gemeinschaft/Gesellschaft* framework as a useful way to characterize reforms. Through the lens of this framework, reforms may be viewed as differing in whether they reflect *Gemeinschaft* or *Gesellschaft* values for schools. Most first-wave reforms are distinctly *gesellschaftlich* in that they reflect a presumed linkage between national economic competitiveness and education. In this view, a better-educated work force is considered crucial to productivity and economic competition (Kirst, 1990), and the schools are considered an appropriate tool for training this work force. This economic impetus for reform is beautifully illustrated in the following quote from an article that appeared in *Phi Delta Kappan*:

> Other nations with which America currently competes *in the world marketplace* have education systems that already produce *higher levels of measured achievement* than ours. If we continue on our present course, the situation will surely get much worse. Thus the *need for education reform* is clear. (Hoyt, 1991, p. 453; emphasis added)

This assumed link between economic competitiveness and schooling improvement is so embedded in the American psyche that it is seldom questioned, even by educators. It, and the reforms based on it, are a natural extension of the "drift to *Gesellschaft*" we traced in the previous chapter.

In contrast, many other reforms appear to reflect *Gemeinschaft* values for schools. These reforms focus not on the *Gesellschaft* value of economic competitiveness, but more on the *Gemeinschaft* values of community connections and a safe and nurturing environment for children. Included here are reforms concerned with strengthening connections between school and community, such as local governance models that involve community members, other types of parent-involvement programs, and children's service coordination. Also included in the *Gemeinschaft* category would be initiatives aimed at making schools themselves more community-like, though these initiatives are seldom formalized into reform policies. Basically, the schools-*as*-community movement is much discussed in the literature, but is not embodied in any systematic way in state reform initiatives; however, there have been quite a few independent initiatives to recreate schools as communities.

In this chapter, we will begin to explore the promise of reforms aimed at restoring the *Gemeinschaft/Gesellschaft* balance in schools. Here, we will consider reforms aimed at school-community connections. In Chapter 6 we will turn to schools as community.

REFORMS FOCUSED ON
SCHOOL-COMMUNITY CONNECTIONS

Reforms focused on school-community connections aim in general to improve educational outcomes for children by strengthening the links among schools, parents, and community agencies. These efforts fall into three majors categories: those that involve parents and community members in school governance, other types of parent-involvement programs (e.g., instructional partnerships), and children's service coordination (Crowson & Boyd, 1993). Clearly, these reforms vary in terms of the goals of initiating stakeholders and the mechanisms used to achieve these goals. Parent involvement in school governance often has been politically motivated, as state legislators respond to pressure from parent groups for more say in local school governance. In contrast, children's service coordination is related to a broader evolution within the social service field and is partly motivated by an economic need for efficiency in delivery of service. These various movements, then, present a somewhat fragmented or incoherent picture in regard to rebuilding connections between school and community.

In this chapter, we want to examine these different fragments of the community-connections reform movement. It is not our goal here to provide a comprehensive review of these reforms, but to focus on those that are most widely implemented and therefore most representative of the community-connections movement. In the following sections, we will look at school-based management as the typical mechanism for involving parents and community members in school governance, other types of parent involvement programs, and children's service coordination involving schools. As we examine these topics, we will be looking for relevant patterns that emerge from recent literature and research, as illustrated by specific cases when appropriate. What these reforms promise they may not be able to deliver unless they address some of the underlying causes of the "drift to *Gesellschaft*" that we explored in Chapter 4.

SCHOOL-BASED MANAGEMENT

School-based management (SBM) is a prominent and persistent reform proposal related to a broader movement to decentralize school governance. This movement is nothing new. It has resurfaced at various times in the history of American education for a variety of reasons (Hess, 1991; Malen, Ogawa, & Kranz, 1990; Weise & Murphy, 1995a, 1995b). However, in the form of SBM, decentralization has enjoyed an unprecedented resurgence within recent years. One reason for its current popularity is educators' tendency to emulate successful business practices. Here, SBM parallels the trend toward participative management in business, which is "sweeping across the American business community" (Hess, 1991, p. 117). Another reason for SBM's popularity springs directly from school-effectiveness research, which found that local, school-site autonomy in addressing educational problems is associated with effectiveness (Purkey & Smith, 1983). Whatever the basis for its current resurgence, one of the hopes for SBM is that it will help reconnect schools with communities, to make schools "more responsive to the communities, families and students they serve" (Bryk, Easton, Kerbow, Rollow, & Sebring, 1993, p. 2). Lewis (1993) explains this rationale:

> If the community (meaning the people who lived near the school) and the parents of school-age children had more voice in the schooling enterprise, then there would be more parental satisfaction with the schools and more commitment to the educational process. . . . The democratization of the governance process and the representation of parental and community interests would lead to improved schooling. (p. 91)

Yet, in examining the SBM movement, it is clear that only a narrow range of currently implemented SBM initiatives offer any real promise

here. Most SBM models simply realign decision making *within* the
organization, without meaningful involvement by community members. In some cases, decision-making authority is shifted from the central office to the school principal, while in others teachers are included
as well. Murphy and Beck (1995) call these two types of SBM "administrative control" and "professional control" respectively. Both these
models are simply "one level of bureaucracy . . . juxtaposed for another" (Sackney & Kibski, as cited in Murphy & Beck, 1995, p. 177), an
approach that holds little promise for impacting school-community
connections.

In contrast, a third model for SBM is "community control," which
purportedly "shifts power from professional educators and the board of
education to parent and community groups not previously involved in
school governance" (Wohlstetter & Odden, 1992, p. 533). Murphy and
Beck (1995) point out that this is the *least commonly implemented*
version of SBM.

We will limit our discussion here to this third type of SBM—
community control—because it is the only type that holds any promise for community connections. Given that this is the least commonly
implemented version of SBM, we are restricted to a narrow range of
initiatives and relevant literature. We turn first to the Chicago reform,
which is frequently touted as the best exemplar of community control
of schools through school-based management.

The Chicago Reform and Community Connections

> The Chicago school reform effort is the largest and most radical SBM
> experiment in the United States in granting authority to local parents,
> community representatives, and school professionals as a strategy for im-
> proving student achievement. (Hess, 1995, p. 25)

Few would argue with this statement by G. Alfred Hess, Jr., the direc-
tor of the Chicago Panel on School Policy, who has studied the Chicago reform for over 10 years and published two books on its history
(Hess, 1991; 1995). Though SBM has been incorporated into numerous
statewide reforms (e.g., Kentucky, Oregon, Texas, and Washington)
and large urban districts (e.g., Dade County, Florida; Los Angeles;
Rochester, New York), Chicago remains the best-known example of
mandated SBM in a large district. Elmore (1991) argues that Chicago's
reform is "more ambitious—some would say more radical—than any
other current reform in its departure from the established structure of
school organization" (p. vii). With these claims in mind, we explore

here the extent and nature of community involvement in Chicago school governance.

While most school-based reforms have a site council of parents and teachers, Chicago's structure is unique in that parents far outnumber school staff. The mechanism for community involvement in Chicago schools is the local school council (LSC), created as part of the Chicago School Reform Act of 1988 (Hess, 1991, 1995; Moore, 1990). Each LSC is comprised of six parents, two other community representatives, two teachers, and the building principal. At the high schools, one nonvoting student is also a member. Originally, LSC parent representatives were elected by vote of the parents who had children attending the school, while community representatives were elected by residents living within the geographical boundaries of the school enrollment area. However, this "segmented voting pattern" was declared unconstitutional by the Illinois Supreme Court in 1990 as a violation of the constitutional provision for "one person–one vote." Now, both parent and community LSC representatives are jointly elected by parents and community members.

The LSCs have three major responsibilities: to adopt a school improvement plan, to adopt a building budget to implement that plan based on a lump-sum allocation, and to select the school principal (Moore, 1990). In Hess's (1991) view,

> The school reform act vested formal control in the new local school councils, turning them from being "advisors" with some power into being "deciders" with ultimate authority on most issues. (p. 151)

Since its inception, the Chicago reform has had a bumpy history fraught with political, financial, and legal challenges. The Supreme Court decision mentioned above resulted from a suit brought by the Chicago Principals Association, which unsuccessfully argued that LSCs' authority to terminate principals' contracts was a violation of tenure provision. In 1991, further difficulties occurred when the Chicago school system was racked by financial crisis. Last-minute budget cuts forced seven schools to close and many teachers and students to be reassigned. A second major financial crisis occurred in 1993 when the district's budget was found to be $200 million out of balance, and 1,000 teachers were laid off. "The chaos engendered by the fiscal instability undermined much of the progress made during the previous 4 years of reform" (Hess, 1995, p. 112).

Most recently, Mayor Richard M. Daley was given additional power by the legislature to "work with troubled schools to install new leadership or even close troubled schools" (Applebome, 1995, p. B6). While these crises have created the impression in the broader educational community that Chicago's reform is faltering, if not failing altogether, many aspects remain intact. Most relevant to our present discussion, the local school councils have continued to operate throughout the 7 years of the reform's history (Hess, 1995).

As stated earlier, the Chicago SBM plan is considered unique in giving more LSC votes to parent and community members than to the professional staff and in granting to the LSCs programmatic, budgetary, and personnel control. This configuration is supposed to shift the balance of control to the local community. However, when one looks more closely at the LSC decision-making structure and the emerging data on participation rates and decision domains (Bryk et al., 1993; Hess, 1995), patterns of continued strong professional influence begin to surface.

First, the LSC decision-making structure left many important prerogatives in the hands of the principal and teachers. Although the LSC in each school was charged with approving a "school-improvement plan," primary responsibility for developing the plan was vested in the principal as advised by the Professional Personnel Advisory Committee (PPAC), made up of certified classroom teachers. Further, building principals retained the right to select teachers and other key personnel, and to develop the budget for LSC approval. As Hess (1991) states:

> The basic structure of the LSC puts the initiative on educational and budgetary matters in the hands of the professionals: foremost, the principal in consultation with the advisory committee of teachers (PPAC). (p. 160)

Thus, while the LSC is vested with authority to *approve* the plan and the budget, and parent/community votes outnumber educator votes, the initiative to *develop and articulate* the plan and budget is in the hands of the professionals. This structure suggests that influence over the educational program is heavily weighted toward the professionals. As Hess's words suggest, it is understood that the "lay" members of the LSC serve as monitors rather than initiators of the school program.

Data on LSC participation rates in different decision domains during the first two years of the reform support this inference (Hess, 1995). Principals participated more frequently than any other LSC members, addressing about two-thirds of all items discussed at LSC meetings, and speaking most frequently about the school program. The LSC chairperson (always a parent) participated in about half the discussions of LSC organizational issues, building and safety items, and personnel issues, while other parents (not the chair) "rarely spoke to any of the issues" (p. 61). Community members, as well, were most likely to be heard on building and safety issues and on LSC organizational matters, and less frequently on school programs. The most frequently discussed topic overall was the school's program (29%), with LSC organizational topics next most frequently on the agenda (28%). Thus, considering that school program was the most frequently discussed item and that principals dominated this topic, which parents seldom addressed, it is clear that in operation, influence within the LSC on the core issue of school program was heavily weighted to the professionals.

The school improvement plans (SIPs) developed by each LSC were another opportunity for community involvement in shaping the school's program, although, as we mentioned before, educators took the lead in developing the SIPs. In examining 14 of these plans in depth, Hess (1995) found that most of the initiatives were very conservative "add-ons" to the regular program, often focusing on special-needs students. Hess concluded that most SIPs "were not likely to create radical change in the schools . . . they relied more on adding small increments than on making radical changes" (p. 68). Adding to this picture, Bryk and his colleagues (1993) reported the results of studies conducted by the Consortium on Chicago School Research. Their research focused on the 85% of Chicago elementary schools performing below national norms. After 4 years of reform, Bryk concluded that 39% to 46% of these schools still operated under "consolidated principal power," with parents not broadly participating in decision making.

On the other hand, there is some limited data indicating that LSCs do promote parent involvement in core curriculum issues. Blackledge (1995), a British educator, interviewed parents and educators at Chicago's Woodland Park Elementary School. Here he found that parents, primarily through the LSC, had started a successful parent involvement program and contributed to changes in the curriculum, including an enhanced bilingual educational program that relies on bilingual parent volunteers. Blackledge concludes that "in some Chicago schools minority group parents are making the most of their new powers to bring about valuable changes in their children's schools" (p. 313).

In sum, this brief review of Chicago's reform suggests that it brought only modest changes to the hierarchical structure of schools and that professionals (principals and teachers) retained a high level of influence on the school's core program through development of the school improvement plans and budgets, and through participation in LSCs. Changes in school programs were modest, not "radical," and tended to be add-ons to the school's program. To date, then, the Chicago SBM reform presents a picture of a modest governance reform that opens the door to participation by community members in decision domains that have had limited impact on the school's core program.

Other Research on SBM

The findings from Chicago are complemented by other research studies and comprehensive reviews of the literature on SBM (Malen et al., 1990; Murphy & Beck, 1995; Wohlstetter & Odden, 1992). A more typical SBM model, less "radical" than Chicago's reform but still representing a community-control model, was studied by Malen and Ogawa (1988) in Salt Lake City. According to Malen and Ogawa, Salt Lake City represented a "critical case" for SBM because it included several features that give SBM the best chance for success in promoting shared governance with the community. These included (1) site councils with broad jurisdiction for policy decisions; (2) parity provisions that "make principals, teachers, and parents equal partners with equal power" (p. 253); and (3) training in group decision making for site council members.

Despite these features, Malen and Ogawa (1988) found that meaningful shared governance with community members did not occur in Salt Lake City. They found that parents on the site councils did not wield significant influence on policy decisions in core areas. Rather, the site councils became "ancillary advisors and pro forma endorsers" (p. 256) of decisions made by the "professionals," primarily the school principals. According to Malen and Ogawa, the traditional influence relationships were not disturbed by SBM in Salt Lake City because (1) parent members were "invited" to be members, rather than being elected by constituent community groups, and tended to be "traditional supporters of the schools" (p. 260); (2) professionals retained control over resources and were still seen as "experts" by parents; and (3) norms of civility led council members to avoid conflict by "confining agendas to marginal matters" (p. 264). As in Chicago, traditional patterns of professional influence served as a barrier to meaningful community involvement.

Recent reviews of the research on SBM contribute to this picture. Malen, Ogawa, and Kranz (1990) conducted a case study of the SBM literature to determine what was known about SBM as a reform. They concluded that "there is little evidence that school-based management alters [professional/patron] influence relationships" (p. 324). In fact, they found evidence that SBM tends to maintain these influence relationships by serving as a "buffer," a vehicle "that principals and professionals can use to buffer themselves from the repercussions of potentially divisive issues . . . by sharing responsibility for these decisions with stakeholders" (p. 307). Wohlstetter and Odden (1992), in a later review of the research, concluded that SBM "did not change authority relationships significantly, largely because . . . few governance changes were made" (p. 533). Finally, Murphy and Beck (1995), in the most recent and comprehensive review of SBM, reached a number of similar conclusions. Though research suggests that SBM does enhance *teacher* involvement in decision making, studies over the last 10 years on SBM's capacity to open up school systems to "outsiders" are "pessimistic" (p. 142).

Summary

Our analysis of the promise of SBM in regard to school-community connections is tempered by two important limitations: (1) Valid generalizable conclusions about SBM cannot be drawn from the existing research base, which is characterized by noncomparability of cases and the failure of researchers to consider alternative explanations for outcomes attributed to SBM (Malen, Ogawa, & Kranz, 1990; Murphy & Beck, 1995); and (2) the cited reviews of research include the gamut of SBM models, not just community control models. However, we are comfortable in pointing out some indicators from the literature and research that are available:

1. Most implemented models of SBM hold little promise for community connections because they represent simple shifts of decision-making authority within the existing hierarchy. In its typical manifestation, SBM may be a "bureaucratic" solution to problems that shifts authority and accountability within the system.
2. Community control models of SBM, though seldom implemented, theoretically hold some promise for community connections. However, even in its most "radical" form as manifested in Chicago, community-control SBM has had only moderate impact on the bureaucratic, hierarchical structure of the school organization and on the traditional influence relationships among parents/community members and professionals.
3. Parent/community representatives on SBM councils may not represent authentic "subcommunities" served by the school.

This is especially true in the most typical SBM models in which parent members may be "invited" to participate or are elected by traditional school support groups such as the Parent Teacher Association (PTA). Even in Chicago, the election process for parent/community representatives assumes that "at large" voting will result in election of community members who truly represent their constituencies. However, in our view, there is no reason to believe that subcommunities (e.g., ethnic enclaves) will be fairly represented on these councils.

4. Because of the participation patterns and agenda setting by school professionals, the actions of SBM councils typically have little impact on the school's core program and mission.

Thus, there is ample evidence that SBM as currently conceptualized and typically implemented has little impact on the underlying causes of weak school-community connections. Paradoxically, SBM may be in some cases an elaboration of the school's bureaucracy, in our analysis one of the major barriers to school-community connections. As Malen and Ogawa (1988) state:

> The research casts doubt on the efficacy of site-based governance as a reform strategy, or, more precisely, it underscores the difficulty of establishing arrangements that will fundamentally alter principal, teacher, and parent influence relationships. (p. 266)

This does not mean that the SBM *concept* does not have the potential to impact school-community connections over time. There is some evidence that more "radical" versions of SBM may lead to greater community involvement in school governance over time and to some impact on the school's core program (Blackledge, 1995; Bryk et al., 1993; Hess, 1995). It is possible that SBM, as typically implemented, has "simply not been given a full or fair test" (Malen et al., 1990, p. 327). It is also possible that SBM, as a "fragment" of the community-connections movement, has limited impact unless it is joined with other community-connections initiatives in a more holistic approach.

COORDINATED SERVICES FOR CHILDREN

"Children's service coordination" is the label we are using for an array of contemporary efforts to link schools with other social service agencies to improve services to children. Other terms often used are "services integration," "school-linked services," and "interagency collaboration." This thrust toward service coordination involving schools is part of a broader social service movement toward collaboration across agencies. This movement has been spurred by two primary developments: the increasing need for family support services due to worsening conditions associated with poverty, and the concomitant reduction in available resources to meet these needs. Advocates for coordination argue that it will reduce the fragmentation within the system, thereby enhancing the effectiveness of services while leading to greater economic efficiency (Gardner, 1990; Kirst & McLaughlin, 1990). In regard to schools, a related hope is to enhance success in school for "at-risk" students whose lives are affected by various social problems (Furman & Merz, 1996).

Crowson and Boyd (1993) outline three basic structures for service coordination involving schools: "A school-based approach (with the school as the dominant player), a school-linked strategy (with the school as a collegial partner), and a community-based approach (with the school as a lesser player)" (p. 143). Knapp (1995) provides a further elaboration, listing at least seven different "meanings" for coordinated services. These range from simply improving the referral mechanisms among agencies, including schools, to joint planning and execution of services across agencies.

Service coordination has been included in several states' reform initiatives such as those in California, Colorado, Kentucky, and New Jersey (First, Curcio, & Young, 1994) and a number of independent projects have been spurred by foundation grants. Several models are becoming known for their exemplary practices or positive outcomes. These include California's Healthy Start (White, 1994), the School of the Future project in Texas (Arvey & Tijerina, 1995), and A Child's Place, which serves homeless children in North Carolina (Mickelson, Yon, & Carlton-LaNey, 1995). However, the research base on coordination remains thin. There have been few in-depth evaluations of these initiatives, and what little is known points to a variety of implementation problems and institutional barriers (Crowson & Boyd, 1995; Gray, 1995; Kirst, 1991), including legal regulations that impede efficient coordination, "turf battles" among different agencies, and the differing professional backgrounds of agency workers. A number of writers point out the methodological problems in evaluating these efforts, including that they are complex and emergent, and involve a wide range of outcomes (Knapp, 1995; Rigsby, 1995; Wang, Haertel, & Walberg, 1995). Needless to say, the specific impact of service coordination on school-community connections has *not* been systematically studied, nor have the dynamics of collaboration been as extensively studied as those of school-based management.

However, when one examines the service coordination literature, some relevant themes emerge. First, school involvement in service coordination involves new professional roles in schools and the expansion of the school bureaucracy. While one of the aims of coordination is greater overall efficiency in delivery of services, the irony is that in most schools, coordinating services and communicating with other agencies involves either new roles for existing staff (Melaville & Blank, 1991) or new positions to be added. This coordination role is seen by some as a new "profession" in the schools (Crowson & Boyd, 1993; Gardner, 1994) requiring specialized training (Knapp et al., 1994). There is no suggestion in the literature that service coordination has any impact on the existing hierarchical structure and authority relationships within the school. In fact, this theme suggests that engaging in coordination often involves an elaboration of the school's bureaucracy.

Supporting the conclusion that coordination involves new roles and organizational elaborations, a second theme in the literature is that additional resources are needed to support it (Cunningham, 1990). Often, new sources of money are required to even begin collaborative efforts (Kirst & McLaughlin, 1990). A lack of adequate resources has been cited frequently as a barrier or a cause of failure of service coordination projects (Hord, 1986).

A third theme is the pervasiveness throughout the literature of the language of "professionals" providing "services" to "clients" (Crowson & Boyd, 1993; Hodgkinson, 1989). Frequent references are made to identifying the clients to be "targeted" for services, and, as mentioned above, service coordinators within schools may be seen as constituting a new profession. These three themes suggest a bureaucratic, *gesellschaftlich* flavor to the coordination reform. They reflect a bureaucratic response to solving problems through increased specialization and growth of the organization (Perrow, 1970).

A recent study on service coordination reflects these themes. Smrekar (1996) conducted an in-depth qualitative study of two Family Resource Centers established under the Kentucky Education Reform Act of 1990. These centers are quite typical of the service coordination movement and represent the "school-based" approach outlined by Crowson and Boyd (1993). The Family Resource Centers are housed in schools, supported by state grant money, and managed by a coordinator. Their purpose is to "connect families with the services necessary to meet basic needs" (p. 5), including child care, health services, and adult education.

Smrekar (1996) found that the centers focused on "crisis intervention" for students, helping them secure immediately needed services. Educators deeply appreciated this "problem-solving" approach to children's needs and a number of "success stories" for individual children were offered. At the same time, the fundamental disconnection between the schools and families continued. As Smrekar states, "the family resource centers fail to fundamentally re-order the character and content of family-school interactions in terms of deeper interactions between parents and teachers" (p. 21). Smrekar identifies several reasons for the continued disconnection. First, the centers served as a convenient "dumping ground" for the most serious problems of students and their families so that center staff were continually involved in time-consuming crisis management rather than in outreach programs to parents. Second, parents saw the center as independent from the school; their sense of the school itself did not change. Parent education programs, which parents associated with "school," had very poor attendance, while participation rates related to other services were high. Third, since centers served as crisis-management mediators between teachers and families, the informal relationship between teachers and parents was unaffected. As Smrekar points out, it is only through *direct* contact between teachers and parents that understanding and cooperation between school and families are increased.

Summary

Service coordination programs differ widely from setting to setting, and there have been several calls for more "personalization" in providing these services to families (e.g., Kirst & McLaughlin, 1990). However, the Smrekar (1996) study and the themes in the literature illustrate some overall cautions in considering service coordination as a community-connections reform. It is primarily a connection *among professionals* across community agencies, rather than between schools and community members. It is an elaboration of the school's structure rather than a way to change the bureaucratic hierarchy, which is a source of intimidation to parents. It has little impact on the school's mission, real or perceived, since it is unrelated to the core educational program, and parents often view the services received as independent of the school itself.

Thus, as it is typically implemented, children's service coordination fails to address the underlying issues related to school-community connections, according to our analysis. In fact, in our view, it can hardly be termed a school-community connection reform. Though it may provide needed services to children, it is primarily a mechanism for "professional-professional" connections to increase efficiency and effectiveness in delivery of these services.

PARENT-INVOLVEMENT PROGRAMS

Where SBM focuses on parent/community involvement in school *governance*, a variety of other parent-involvement initiatives have been implemented or proposed that do not focus on governance per se, but that are also attempts to strengthen school-community connections. Often these are efforts to create "instructional partnerships" between educators and parents (Crowson & Boyd, 1993). In fact, the currently popular term for these efforts is "home-school partnerships" (Epstein, 1995; Swap, 1993), a term we will use here interchangeably with "parent involvement." Parent involvement in schools is nothing new. Among the traditional mechanisms for parent participation are Parent Teacher Associations, parent advisory committees, and school volunteering programs. The problem with these traditional mechanisms in regard to school-community connections is that the school maintains control and parents continue in less influential roles (Epstein, 1995; Henry, 1996; Swap, 1993). However, as part of the broader decentralization movement in education, new avenues for school-parent collaboration focusing on "partnerships" are being advocated and explored, and a growing research base indicates a positive relationship between these efforts and children's educational outcomes (Mannan & Blackwell, 1992; Swap, 1993). Epstein captures the rationale for these programs:

> They can improve school programs and school climate, provide family services and support, increase parents' skills and leadership, connect families with others in the school and in the community, and help teachers with their work. However, the main reason to create such partnerships is to help all youngsters succeed in school and in later life. (p. 701)

Swap (1993) adds yet another argument, which echoes the plea of the critical humanists (see Chapter 4) for a new democratic "mission" for schools:

> Home-school partnerships in diverse communities are contributing to the creation of better schools that are both microcosms and forerunners of a new multicultural, multiracial democracy in America. (p. xiii)

Clearly, a primary hope for parent-involvement programs is the enhancement of school-community connections.

Models of Home-School Partnerships

Swap (1993) provides a framework to categorize parent involvement programs based on the type of *relationships* that prevail between educators and parents, "each of which is defined by a different set of goals, assumptions, attitudes, behaviors, and strategies" (p. 28). Swap delineates four "models" for these relationships: the protective model, the school-to-home transmission model, the curriculum enrichment model, and the partnership model. Among these four the protective model is not of interest here. Although it is the *dominant* model for home-school *relationships*, according to Swap, it does not reflect the current movement toward enhanced school-home *partnerships*; rather, it reflects the traditional separation between home and school based in the school's need to "buffer" or "protect" itself from interference by parents. Parent involvement in such a model would go no further than the traditional mechanisms of PTA, parent conferences, and limited volunteering opportunities.

Swap's (1993) other three models all reflect proactive efforts to involve parents in schooling. In the *school-to-home transmission model*, educators recognize the important role that parents play in their children's education and seek to enlist parents' support for the school's objectives. Some typical activities here would be a high level of communication from school to home (e.g., through newsletters or "homework hotlines"), active volunteer programs, and workshops for parents. Swap points out that most schools' parent-involvement programs are based on this model.

In contrast, the *curriculum enrichment model* seeks to directly involve parents in shaping the school's curriculum. It assumes that a curriculum shaped by parent input is more likely to reflect the values of the families represented in the school. As would be expected, a major focus in this approach is a multicultural curriculum that reflects the cultural heritage of the students. Though this model does emphasize "reciprocal" interactions between parents and educators, it is restricted to the areas of curriculum and instruction.

In the fourth model, the *partnership model*, "collaborative relationships between home and school permeate all areas of school culture" (Swap, 1993, p. 46). The partnership model differs from the school-to-home transmission model in emphasizing two-way communication and collaborative problem solving with parents. It differs from the curriculum enrichment model in going beyond curriculum and instruction to take in "all areas" of the school program. The goal is for educators and parents to work together toward a mission that is jointly defined.

Swap's (1993) categories are analytically useful for considering the promise of home-school partnerships in regard to school-community connections. We will use the school-to-home transmission model and the partnership model as overarching categories for examining home-school partnership initiatives. We will not refer to the curriculum enrichment model separately, because, in our view, it is a subtype of the partnership model, restricted to one aspect of schooling.

School-to-Home Transmission Model for Parent Involvement. The basic assumption of the school-to-home transmission model is that parents have an important responsibility to help their children succeed in school, according to the school's expectations and standards. Parents can fulfill this responsibility by preparing their children to begin school and supporting their children in school by providing a healthy home environment, appropriate clothing and supplies, a space to do homework, and so on. Most important is that parents support the expectations and values of the school by training their children in the attitudes and skills associated with school success. In the school-to-home model, "it is school personnel who define goals and programs. Two-way communication is not sought because the goal is for parents to understand and support the school's objectives" (Swap, 1993, p. 30). This perspective certainly prevails in the American public school system.

Appropriate activities for parent involvement under the school-to-home transmission model then flow from this basic assumption. Schools should communicate effectively with parents regarding the school's program and expectations. Parents should be active supporters of the school through participating as volunteers in the classroom and elsewhere. Parents should be available and willing to engage in homework assignments with their children. And, if parents lack the background, skills, and resources to train their children appropriately, then the school should provide training to the parents. The focus here is on correcting deficits in parents' capabilities.

Henry (1996) provides a recent, in-depth ethnographic study of parent involvement in a "typical" school district that illustrates the school-to-home transmission model. "Robertson," the district Henry studied, is a small city district in a university town in the Northwest. In this district, where "teachers and administrators believe they are being inclusive," there was much rhetoric about parent involvement spurred by the recent implementation of school-based management. However, the level and type of parent involvement activities were conservative and traditional. These included a great deal of communication from school to home in the form of district newsletters, school building newsletters, and communication from individual teachers. Teachers in the high school had their own phones and used them to call parents with concerns about individual students. At the middle school, a computerized telephone system allowed parents to call in for homework assignments and other announcements. Parent volunteers were actively sought in some schools as classroom aides or guest speakers, but avoided "like the plague" in others because they "get in the way" of teaching. In addition, two of the elementary schools sponsored parent education programs for parents "needing some assistance."

Henry's (1996) analysis uncovered a number of themes related to parent-school relationships in Robertson. Despite the heightened rhetoric around parent involvement and collaboration, there was a continued "distancing" between parents and schools. The professional culture of the school operated on assumptions that "teachers should teach and parents should parent" (p. 62) and that educators should have professional autonomy in their work. Administrators retained strong authority and viewed their work with the community as "managing" community relations. Parents often felt unwelcome in the schools and intimidated by the school's bureaucracy. Minority parents, in particular, were not visible in the schools. Those parents who did volunteer—typically women—often felt used by the school and taken for granted. Formal events such as open house sometimes "took on a ritualistic 'performance' character, serving a function of recognizing teachers and parents and their separate roles, without dispelling either group's distrust of the other, or moving into real problem solving" (p. 52). Henry concludes:

> The participants in this study at Robertson School District showed over and over, in various ways, that schools are segmented, hierarchical, bureaucratic organizations and that despite moves toward site-based management and shared decision making, and despite a desire for collaborative partnerships, the mindset and the technology continue to divide teachers as "professionals" from parents as "lay" people. (p. 178)

The Henry (1996) study illustrates that the school-to-home transmission model for parent involvement may do little to bridge the gap between school and community. In particular, the model assumes that the school's mission as embodied in its program and expectations for students is "correct" and that parents need only support it. Parents are not invited to reshape this mission. Swap (1993) points out that this is particularly problematic when there is a misfit between the school's culture and the community's culture.

Partnership Model for Parent Involvement. In contrast to the school-to-home transmission model, the partnership model involves "long-term commitments, mutual respect, widespread involvement of families and educators in many levels of activities, and sharing of planning and decision-making responsibilities" (Swap, 1993, p. 47). The major assumptions behind the model are that schools should be "re-visioned" to meet current challenges, they should be completely re-structured in line with the new vision, and collaboration between parents and educators is necessary to accomplish this. Swap outlines four primary components of the partnership model: (1) *Two-way communication* between parents and educators to create "a negotiated set of joint expectations for children and the school" (p. 58); (2) *mutual responsibility* between parents and educators to enhance learning for students; (3) *mutual support activities* such as parent education programs provided by the school and volunteering by parents to support school programs; and (4) *joint decision making* between parents and educators. In short, the partnership model involves a complete rethinking of the traditional relationship between schools and parents.

Clearly, the partnership model connotes a broader approach to school-community connections that involves parent participation in school governance (e.g., SBM) as well as other forms of parent involvement. The two examples provided by Swap (1993)—Levin's Accelerated Schools Model and Comer's School Development Program—bear this out. Levin's model involves "high levels" of parent involvement; parents are involved in the school's steering committee (a form of SBM), as volunteers, and in a variety of activities to support the program's "accelerated" curriculum. Comer's model focuses on three levels of parent involvement that, like Levin's, take in school governance, volunteering, and instructional-support activities. The Comer model also includes "children's service coordination" in that Comer schools are to serve as a community hub for coordinating social services to families. It should be noted here that both the Levin and Comer models are fairly elaborate and were developed to meet the critical needs of at-risk student populations in failing urban schools.

Here we are faced with an analytical dilemma. As more holistic approaches, the Levin and Comer models take in school *as* community as well as many avenues for school-community connections. In fact, Comer's model is frequently touted as a "community-building" approach in individual schools (Comer, Haynes, Joyner, & Ben-Avie, 1996). While we agree that these models may be legitimate examples in matching Swap's criteria for the partnership model, parent involvement is only part of the reform picture they offer. They may also be viewed as intending to reshape the school *as* community. We chose, therefore, to examine Comer's model in the next chapter, as an example of holistic reforms aimed at both recreating the school as a community and at community connections. We begin to see, however, that there is a great deal of overlap between school-community connections and school *as* community within initiatives that are more holistic in approach.

Summary

Using Swap's (1993) models helps us see some major points about parent involvement that are very useful in our analysis. It is the philosophy or assumptions behind the parent-involvement program that are important, not the structure, scope, or nature of specific activities. *When the assumption is that the school's program is "correct"* and need only be supported by parents to be successful (as in the school-to-home transmission model), the *Gesellschaft* mission of the school is not challenged or modified. The hierarchical structure of the school is not disturbed, and the school culture does not connect with subcommunities. Since *most* parent-involvement programs are of this type, they can be expected to have little impact on school-community connections. *When the assumption is that the school's program is open to negotiation with parents* (as suggested in the partnership model), there is likely to be more opportunity to involve community members in re-creating the program and mission, in challenging the school's hierarchical structure, and in developing authentic connections between school and subcommunities.

THE PROMISE OF COMMUNITY-CONNECTIONS REFORMS

We have seen in this overview that individual reforms address fragments of the community-connections issue. School-based management approaches the issue from the angle of formal school governance. While it theoretically "decentralizes" governance, paradoxically it is often an elaboration of the school's own bureaucracy with little impact on traditional influence relationships. Children's service coordination addresses another fragment—the isolation of the school as a social service agency from other agencies in the community. In practice, service coordination involves school professionals connecting with other professionals rather than with parents and other community members. In fact, we think it is a stretch to consider service coordination a community-connections reform. Parent-involvement efforts, for the most part, address a third fragment of the picture—the common lack of parent participation in their children's education, or, in the worst case, the alienation of parents from schools. While purportedly aimed at direct collaboration between the school and parents, many parent-involvement programs remain at a shallow level, and often may be a mechanism to get parent support for the school-determined program.

We see a central problem with this fragmented approach to community connections. Because the individual reforms are usually not connected to each other in a meaningful way, they end up tinkering around the margins of the school-community interface rather than getting at the core, underlying issues. When these reforms are implemented in isolation, the centralized, bureaucratic school structure remains practically untouched, few efforts are made to identify and collaborate with authentic subcommunities, and the school's underlying *gesellschaftich* mission is not transformed.

When these approaches begin to come together in a more comprehensive way, as suggested by Swap's (1993) conceptualization of the partnership model for home-school relationships, there appears to be more promise for enhanced school-community connections. And here, the line between school-community connections and school *as* community begins to blur.

6

The Promise of Reform:
School as Community

In modern times the school has been solidly ensconced in the
gesellschaft *camp . . . with unhappy results. It is time that*
the school was moved from the gesellschaft *side of the ledger*
to the gemeinschaft *side. It is time that the metaphor for*
school was changed from formal organization to community.
— *Sergiovanni,* Building Community in Schools

In this chapter we turn to a set of reforms that attempt to reshape
schools so they become communities in themselves. While most of
the writers that we consider would acknowledge the importance of
external relations, they all advocate that attention be focused on the
nature of the school itself. They consider variously the individual
classroom, the whole school, or subunits such as departments or
"schools within a school," but all advocate that the school organization
become more community-like.

ORIGINS AND RATIONALE FOR SCHOOL AS COMMUNITY

The idea of the school as community grew simultaneously out of several bodies of research: effective-schools research, "teacher's work" literature, and the literature on caring. Each of these has contributed a
different definition of community and focuses on slightly different
aspects. In the next sections, we consider each of these.

School-Effectiveness Research

The school-effectiveness research of the 1970s and 1980s identified
factors common to effective schools, that is, schools that consistently
demonstrate higher student achievement. Most of the qualities identified clustered around order and a focus on academics. However, an-

other set of identified qualities related more to relationships and values. A factor frequently identified was a sense of shared purpose among educators in effective schools, which appeared to be the product of shared values (Purkey & Smith, 1983). Other research specifically identified warm and supportive relationships between teachers and students as an effectiveness factor (Brophy & Good, 1986; Solomon & Kendall, 1979). In general, the effective schools were not harsh, impersonal, or cold; they had a certain quality often identified as "a positive ethos" (Grant, 1988; Hallinger & Murphy, 1986; Lightfoot, 1984; Rutter, Maughan, Mortimore, Ouston, & Smith, 1979; Sizer, 1984).

None of these studies uses the word *community* explicitly in defining these qualities of effective schools, but they have much in common with *Gemeinschaft*, as defined by Tönnies (1887/1957). Positive ethos, for example, often had a sense of parental authority (Lightfoot, 1984), moral purpose (Grant, 1988; Sizer, 1984), and a tendency to value relationships highly (Lightfoot, 1984; Sizer, 1984). Several of these writers mention that effective schools are smaller and less bureaucratic than typical schools. Sizer suggests that effective schools trust teachers and students to make good decisions. In repeated attempts to understand and explore these factors related to values and relationships, researchers eventually came to group them together and label them as a sense of "community" (Rowan, 1990), and to explore the nature of school community and its effects (e.g., Battistich, Solomon, Kim, Watson, & Schaps, 1995; Bryk & Driscoll, 1988).

"Teachers' Work" Literature

Another set of related literature came out of the study of teachers' work in which schools were reported to be lonely, isolating places where teachers have little contact with other adults (e.g., Jackson, 1968; Lortie, 1975). Schools were described as overly bureaucratic and rule-bound in ways that seemed irrelevant to the task at hand. Out of this literature came the ideas, which have become an important piece of the reform literature, of collegiality among teachers and the development of professional community (e.g., Little, 1993; McLaughlin, 1993; Sergiovanni, 1994).

It should be noted that the term *professional community* would be a contradiction in Tönnies's (1887/1957) framework. Professional roles are *gesellschaftlich*, bureaucratic specialties based on specialized expertise, and exist in a hierarchical relationship to others in the workplace, as was pointed out by Parsons (1954). Tönnies discussed a potential *gemeinschaftlich* relationship among co-workers as he described a community of mind that could encompass "members of the same craft . . . united by the cooperation in a common task" (p. 43). In this way craft guilds operated like religions in that "handicraft and art are passed on . . . as if they were dogma and religious mystery" (p. 63). In general, teaching today is more of a profession than an artisan guild; it is learned in an academic setting and tested and licensed by the state. While apprenticeship is important, it is a minor part of most teacher preparation.

Nowhere is the paradoxical notion of professional community more evident than in the work of Newmann and Wehlage (1995). In using a highly *gesellschaftlich* definition of community, they make a connection between professional community and student achievement. They examined data from the School Restructuring Study and the National Educational Longitudinal Study of 1988 and found that schools with higher professional community scores had higher student achievement scores. They identified strong professional community by three factors: clear shared purpose for student learning, collaborative teaching activity, and collective responsibility for student learning. This definition is highly focused on the work of teaching and notably devoid of affinity, belonging, identity, or any of the more global *gemeinschaftlich* qualities. Newmann and Wehlage are really talking about how closely teachers can work together to accomplish their work goals; these are clearly work relationships, not the diffuse, personal relationships of *Gemeinschaft*.

Other writers, however, have taken a broader notion of professional community. Little and McLaughlin, in *Teachers' Work* (1993), defined the qualities in the workplace that support teachers' ability to change and adapt to new challenges in teaching a changing population of students. The qualities they identified were intensity, inclusivity, and orientation to common beliefs. Of intensity, they say "strong ties are rare" (p. 6). Most teachers experienced a fragmentation of their attention among competing aspects of their personal and professional lives; ties to their work colleagues usually paled in comparison with other demands in their lives. With regard to inclusivity, Little and McLaughlin discuss the boundaries of community. They recognize that schools are organized into subunits with varying micropolitics, and that teachers identify with professional groups beyond the schools. Thus the nestedness of communities creates demands on teachers to identify simultaneously with groups at different levels. This poses a real challenge to teachers, and there is some indication that strong identification at the departmental level is more important than identification at the school or district level, suggesting that inclusivity may be an unattainable ideal. Finally, orientation of teacher community (i.e., what beliefs are held in common and whether they are held explicitly or implicitly) was very important in Little and McLaughlin's findings. Individual teachers tended to take on the belief system of a cohesive set of colleagues.

This study is very interesting in that it shows the difficulty of establishing cohesive relationships in large multilevel organizations. Yet it seems that people choose to form bonds even in these ambiguous situations. Moreover, the bonds they form, although not intense or well defined, have the power to shape their belief systems. It would seem that even in this most *gesellschaftlich* of worlds, the modern American high school, teachers find themselves creating *Gemeinschaft*, perhaps the community of mind that Tönnies (1887/1957) described as formed by people "cooperating in a common task" (p. 43).

In *Teachers at Work*, Johnson (1990) found that teachers valued collegiality and most were close to a few other teachers. They thought that bureaucracy and lack of time limited their ability to work with others, but few reported that they felt truly isolated in the workplace. Equally few reported a schoolwide closeness; most felt collegial ties within a department or to teachers in neighboring classrooms. The only schools reporting schoolwide collegiality were small private schools. Johnson urges that schools be established that allow teachers to collaborate and establish collegial relations. The relationships described by Johnson seem pleasant and helpful to teachers, but do not have a very compelling quality. They would seem *gesellschaftlich* in nature in that they focus on the task at hand rather than on the people more broadly.

Tönnies (1887/1957) describes contracts in *Gesellschaft* as a commitment that exists as long as it is needed for an exchange, but ceases to exist when the exchange is completed or becomes impossible to complete. Johnson (1990) seems to recognize this as she calls for collaboration and collegiality, terms conveying a commitment to the task, albeit a mutual commitment, rather than to the individuals. Little and McLaughlin (1993) would appear to intend something more powerful in describing a group that can change an individual's belief system and patterns of behavior. Tönnies would suggest that whether this is a bond of *Gemeinschaft* or *Gesellschaft* depends on the specificity of the bond and its temporary nature. Little and McLaughlin as well as Johnson would probably agree that this is a bond dependent on and limited to the presence of a common task, hence *gesellschaftlich* in nature, but even within that it can meet some bonding needs.

The Literature on Caring

At the same time that the theme of schools as communities was emerging from school-effectiveness research and the teacher work literature, it was growing out of the more philosophically based "caring literature" (Beck, 1994; Noddings, 1984, 1992; Sergiovanni 1992). This group of writers takes a somewhat different tack and suggests that teaching children to care and exhibit moral behavior is a primary goal of the school, and not simply a means for accomplishing other academic goals.

The most prominent work in this field comes from Nel Noddings (1984), who originally wrote on caring in schools as a feminist contribution and an extension of a maternal activity. Since then, it has become a more generalized human responsibility in her own work (Noddings, 1992) and in the work of others such as Boyer (1995) and Sergiovanni (1994).

Noddings (1992) does not mention community as such, but implies community as she calls for caring and continuity. Drawing heavily on Dewey (1902, 1963/1938), she calls for continuity in education to counteract today's disconnected social experience and create schools in which children experience care and learn to care. She then enumerates continuity of purpose, place, people, and curriculum, which defines a whole highly consistent with *Gemeinschaft*. In discussing continuity of place, she prefers small schools where students remain for six years. Noddings also points out the problem of specialization and suggests that the benefits of middle schools may not outweigh the loss of continuity students experience in changing to a building specifically designed for their age group. She sees specialization of professional roles (which we would point out as characteristic of *Gesellschaft*) as also creating discontinuity. She suggests that the continuity of one teacher may be more beneficial than a range of specialized services such as counseling. She would prefer that students and teacher stay together for 3 or more years.

Like Dewey (1963/1938), Noddings (1992) suggests that how schools teach is as important as what they teach. In the long tradition of progressive education, she sees schools as a means for creating a world in which people know how to live together. Her notions of teaching children to care are made clear in her discussions of instruction and curriculum. In this respect her work is much stronger than that of other modern communitarians, who fail to see the internal contradiction in teaching democratic community building through authoritarian means.

Noddings' (1992) work is highly consistent with making schools more *gemeinschaftlich*. She bases her ideal of schooling on the model of a good family and advocates replacing within the school much of what has been lost in modern homes. However, her preoccupation with the goodness of her own affluent, well-educated, two-parent family may seem a little smug and patronizing, causing one to wonder how much thought she has given to the effects of poverty in single-parent families or families in which both parents must hold multiple jobs just to make ends meet. While Noddings discusses the deep social changes that have taken place in the past years, she does not address the causes of change. She suggests that uniform standards and universal curriculum are shallow attempts to deal with these social changes; we would agree, but would point to the inconsistency of the *gesellschaftlich* nature of these solutions to *gemeinschaftlich* problems.

Noddings is a strong advocate for reversing the loss of community in American life today and sees the schools as a major way to accomplish this. Unfortunately, she never really addresses why life has become so uncaring, rootless, and impersonal. Simply to increase "caring" and *Gemeinschaft* without addressing why society and schools have drifted away from these qualities is short-sighted. Unless she recognizes the reasons that *Gesellschaft* solutions are attractive to school people, she will never be rid of what she calls "shallow solutions."

EMPIRICAL RESEARCH INTO ASPECTS OF COMMUNITY

Since the effective-schools research and the work on teachers' professional community, several attempts have been made to operationalize the definition of community so that it might be investigated in an empirical manner.

McMillan and Chavis (1986) describe the factors present in a "sense of community" by reviewing the research of others who have developed scales and observational frameworks for measuring the psychological, emotional, and behavioral dimensions of community. They suggest that four elements are necessary: membership, influence, fulfillment of needs, and emotional connection. Like emotional connection, membership, as they define it, is a traditional *gemeinschaftlich* characteristic that includes boundaries (a sense of members and non-members), a sense of belonging, and a common symbol system. The other two characteristics — influence and fulfillment of needs — are not a part of traditional *Gemeinschaft*, but seem to surface in modern work on community as community members are freer to leave than in the past. These two qualities relate to how members' roles become intertwined in ways that allow them to feel a certain amount of control and satisfaction and seem necessary to retain members in a world that values choice and personal freedom.

Two of the more recent and successful attempts to operationalize the definition of community in schools are those by Bryk and Driscoll (1988) and Battistich et al. (1995). While the Bryk and Driscoll work seems to retain the traditional definition of community, the Battistich et al. study seems to find additional qualities similar to the "influence and fulfillment" of the McMillan and Chavis (1986) study.

Using the High School and Beyond data, Bryk and Driscoll (1988) created a community index and looked for various correlations across teachers' and students' social variables and academic achievement in math. The community index was composed of items indicating shared value system, common agenda of activities, and ethic of caring. They found that high schools exhibiting all these characteristics had higher teacher satisfaction and enjoyment, lower teacher absenteeism, and higher staff morale; lower student absenteeism, class cutting, and dropout rate; less classroom disorder; higher student interest in academics; and higher math achievement. It appears from these data that it is important to exhibit all of their community indicators; the effect on all the dependent variables was much greater than it was if the schools exhibited any of the indicators separately.

Battistich, Solomon, Kim, Watson, and Schaps (1995) say students experience community when their needs for belonging, autonomy, and competence are met at school. They feel acceptance and support; they feel they have an influence on and accept group norms and values. On the basis of questionnaires administered to teachers and students, Battistich et al. (1995) correlated a "sense of community" score and a measure of poverty to students' academic and social attitudes and academic performance. In the findings a high sense of community was associated significantly with students' social and personal attitudes and behaviors, and their academic attitudes, but had little relationship to their academic achievement. Some of their more interesting findings relate to the connection between sense of community and poverty. In general schools with students from low-income families had a lower sense of community, but a sense of community was still related positively with social and personal attitudes. In fact for some variables the effect was strongest in schools serving low-income families.

An examination of the Battistich et al. (1995) definition of community reveals that "belonging" is a part of *Gemeinschaft*, but autonomy and competence are not usual *gemeinschaftlich* qualities. There are many *Gemeinschafts* of kinship and place, in Tönnies's (1887/1957) words, in which the members have little autonomy or sense of competence. In fact the "trapped" or "repressed" sense of members of *Gemeinschafts* has long been one of the factors leading people to leave small towns. Tönnies recognized the fragile nature of *Gemeinschafts* of mind, in which members had the option to choose to leave. Thus it is important to note that Battistich et al. are modifying a traditional definition of community so as to make it more desirable for late 20th century people. In Chapter 3 we saw that there are major challenges to community today, such as choice. When members of a community value choice, the community must face the fact that members may leave the community. Thus it seems reasonable to expect a robust community to be appealing enough and satisfying enough to retain members. In adding autonomy and choice to their definition of community, Battistich et al. have broadened community to define what they call *democratic* community, a particular kind of community they hope to achieve, one that values participation, equality, and inclusiveness. Achieving a democratic community becomes an important goal in itself for schools, whether or not it results in increased academic performance, although the hope and implicit assumption are that academic gains will ultimately be achieved.

Although most of the writing on schools as community is normative, there have been a number of correlational studies, two of which we have reviewed (Battistich et al., 1995; Bryk & Driscoll, 1988). In almost all cases, researchers have reanalyzed existing bodies of data to look for relationships among variables defining community. At this point we can say with some confidence that there is a relationship between community-type variables, as defined in this research, and social satisfaction among teachers and students, but as with the school-effectiveness research in general, there is considerable doubt about cause and effect and even greater doubt about how to implement programs to increase a sense of community in a school. Nevertheless, the stakes are so high and the end so desirable that it seems important to devote thought and effort to look at implementation possibilities.

INCREASING THE SENSE OF COMMUNITY IN SCHOOLS

In the remainder of this chapter, we examine several school reform models that claim to increase a sense of community in schools. These include Ernest Boyer's Basic School, James Comer's School Development Program, Deborah Meier's work at the Central Park East Schools, and Thomas Sergiovanni's proposals for creating community in school. We selected these examples to illustrate the wide range of approaches to community building and the tendency of any one approach to address some aspects of community building to the neglect of others. In each case, we explore the promise of the reform in terms of restoring the *Gemeinschaft/Gesellschaft* balance in schools. We are interested in whether the reform appears to enhance community-like qualities within schools (e.g., trust, personalized relationships, and belongingness) and whether it addresses the underlying causes of the "drift to *Gesellschaft*" we traced in Chapter 4.

Boyer's Basic School

One of the final efforts in Ernest Boyer's work with the Carnegie Foundation was to propose the Basic School (1995). In this outgrowth of his many years of studying the primacy of language to thinking and the importance of human relationships in healthy development, Boyer proposed the Basic School that "is, above all else, a community for learning" (p. 15) for children's early years. He relies on the effective-schools research, his own observations in a wide variety of schools, and the work of writers who comment on social needs of children today to conclude that "community is without question the glue that holds an effective school together" (p. 15). He defines his notion of community by stating the qualities of his Basic School as a place of purpose, communication, fairness, discipline, caring, and celebration.

Boyer (1995) sees community as one of four priorities for the Basic School, along with curriculum coherence, climate, and character. It would be possible to propose a school with these priorities clustered around the concept of community, if community were the real touchstone of the reforms. But as described by Boyer, this multiplicity of purposes quickly loses its connection to community. For example, Boyer describes the need for coordinated social services for children and partnerships with institutions of higher education to maintain a high level of scholarship among teachers in the Basic School. These kinds of collaboration demand high involvement of the staff of the Basic School. No one teacher can be equally involved in such external partnerships and maintain the high internal involvement necessary for the coherent community quality Boyer calls for in the school itself. Inevitably, these partnership tasks will be divided among the staff of the school, resulting in differing internal priorities.

Another example of incipient conflict is in Boyer's (1995) chapter on commitment to character. Stressing the importance of coherent values for school, he suggests that schools adopt seven core virtues to which all will subscribe. While the virtues themselves are not particularly controversial (honesty, respect, self-discipline, compassion, and so forth), controversy is sure to arise in the application of these virtues to everyday situations. For example, the relative importance of one's duty to family responsibilities and school responsibilities varies widely across ethnic groups and sometimes for boys and girls within an ethnic group. Accepting the same set of abstract virtues, different groups within a school will reach honest and responsibly different conclusions. How will the school honor these differences?

A good deal of this confusion stems from Boyer's (1995) methods in establishing the concept of the Basic School. The book in which he describes the Basic School was to be a companion piece to his earlier volumes, *High School: A Report on Secondary Education in America* (1983), *College: The Undergraduate Experience in America* (1987), and *Ready to Learn: A Mandate for the Nation* (1991), his work on infancy and preschool. In reading widely in effective-schools research and visiting sites around the country, he found many "practices that really work" (1995, p. xviii). But no one school did all of these things, nor do we know how many of or in what combination these aspects must exist to get results. In fact we are not sure what the desired results are, except to implement the ideas of effective schooling. The definition of success could vary from community to community as differing emphases are placed on academic or social success. After *The Basic School* was written, a group of schools was formed to implement the ideas, but Boyer included no information on this project in his volume.

Boyer (1995) says his "Basic School is not so much an institution as it is an idea" (p. 3), much in the way Sergiovanni (1994) and McLaughlin (1993) say community is a metaphor for school. Boyer creates an important list of things people are currently doing to improve schools, but without a method of thinking about the ways in which these reforms might conflict or coalesce, it can be nothing more than a list for future research, not a guide to school improvement.

Central Park East Schools

The Central Park East Schools (CPES) in East Harlem, New York City, were started in 1974 with Deborah Meier as co-director. What began as a single small "school within a school" grew into four schools working in collaboration with each other, including a high school program added in 1985 (Meier, 1995). The Central Park East schools are small, alternative "choice" schools within New York City's system; the high school, for example, is part of New York's Alternative High School Division. Although there are no entrance requirements for students, enrollment is limited in each school. The three elementary schools serve 250 students each, while the high school's enrollment is limited to 450. Students are selected by lottery and an effort is made to maintain racial heterogeneity. Most of the students are African-American and Latino (75%), but the schools have been able to "maintain a steady white population" (Meier, 1995, p. 28) that exceeds the average for the district. Most of the students are low-income or poor, and represent a full range of academic abilities.

Meier's work at CPES is based in her commitment to education as a shared public responsibility and as a crucial factor in the survival of democracy. The core issue for Meier and her CPES colleagues is the wasted potential of youth, particularly low-income, inner-city youth — who lose the "power of their ideas" in the intellectually stultifying environments of inner-city schools. Her mission in starting CPES was to create a school that would educate all children well. As Meier (1995) states:

> The question for us was how the children at the bottom of America's social ladder could use their schools to develop rather than stunt their intellectual potential, how to provide at public expense for the least advantaged what the most advantaged bought privately for their own children. (p. 19)

For Meier (1995), a school that meets this charge exhibits several key features: It is a "democratic community" emphasizing collaboration; education is "personalized"; standards are high; the program emphasizes the intellectual development of the students and respects their "ideas." Several features of the Central Park East Schools appear to reflect these ideas. The commitment to democratic community is reflected in the way decisions are made. Collaboration among the faculty is emphasized. There is no "principal" who "supervises" teachers; rather, the school is "staff run" and a "teacher-director" sees to management tasks. In Meier's (1995) words, it was "critical that the school life of adults be democratic. It seemed unlikely that we could foster values of community in our classrooms unless the adults in the school had significant rights over their own workplace" (p. 22).

To have a community, trust is considered essential at CPES — among the teachers, between students and teachers, and between teachers and parents, and these are all intertwined. To build trust,

CPES focuses on an attitude of respect for families and informal collab-oration between school and family. For parents to trust the school, they have to feel that they are respected, that their values are not being undermined by the school. As Meier (1991) states,

> At minimum parents need to know that we will not undermine their authority, their values or their standards. They need to believe that we're not frustrating the aspirations that they have for their kids, nor blaming them for what goes wrong with their kids. (p. 142)

While "eschewing formal teacher/parent co-governance" (Meier, 1995, p. 142), CPES emphasizes openness and accessibility, and the frequency of parent-school contacts. In addition, an effort is made to recruit African-American and Latino staff who can "think like parents" (p. 24). The trust between teachers and parents in turn leads to trust on the part of students: "Children who are suspicious of a school's agenda cannot work up to their potential. For the school to be safe, children needed to know that their parents trusted us. It was that simple" (p. 24). Finally, a key feature for trust among faculty is that they volunteer to teach in the program because they share Meier's philosophy for a school community.

Another key feature of CPES related to both trust and collabora-tion is small size. In the attempt to "personalize" education and build trust among themselves and with students, the size of the schools and the number of students each teacher sees in a day are limited. The secondary school provides a good example. Here the 450 students are divided into three divisions of 150 students; each division is further divided into two "houses" of 75 students, each with its own faculty of four to five teachers who collaborate to plan the program. These arrangements make it possible for CPES secondary school (CPESS) teachers to see about 40 students a day, rather than the 100 or more in a typical large high school.

The high school also illustrates CPES's high academic standards and a focus on intellectual development. The high school's mission statement says, in part: "At CPESS we make an important promise to every student. . . . We promise our students that when they graduate from CPESS, they will have learned to use their minds—and to use their minds well" (Sergiovanni, 1994, p. 38). The high school curricu-lum is organized around two main academic themes—humanities and math-science. Two hours are spent each day in these themes, with additional time allotted for foreign language, physical education, and an "advisory" in which 10 to 15 students meet with one teacher. Students demonstrate their learning through projects and exhibitions rather than through written tests (Meier, 1995).

The Central Park East Schools point to indicators of their success. CPES students score higher than city or state averages on the New York Regency Competency Examinations and a much greater percentage graduate from high school. Further, approximately 90% of students who graduate go on to college. According to Meier (1995), these figures have been consistent for every graduating class to 1995.

Meier (1995) provides convincing evidence that CPES exhibits many features of *Gemeinschaft*, including shared values, a focus on trust, and personalized relationships, and that this model for education produces positive results for students. CPES's promise for creating community in schools lies in demonstrating that it is *possible* for like-minded educators to collaborate in a public school to create a community-like setting for students. Further, the CPES experience provides some lessons for community building: Small size is important; external relationships, for example, with parents, are just as important as intra-school relationships; changes in the hierarchical authority structure are necessary to create trust and collaboration; and a strong common understanding of the school's purpose can become its mission. In attending to these issues, we see CPES as addressing some of the underlying causes of the "drift to *Gesellschaft*" in schools, in particular, the centralized, hierarchical structure of the school and the school's *gesellschaftlich* mission. Further, it appears that CPES's informal approach to parent-school relationships, combined with an ethic of respect for parents' values, is very constructive in bridging the trust gap between school and community. However, CPES restricts its focus here to parents of attending children; it does not reach out to other community groups.

At the same time, discouraging lessons emerge. First, both the student body and the faculty at CPES are *voluntary*. CPES is a school of choice within the New York system, and Meier and her colleagues gathered together to create it because of their shared ideals. This aspect of CPES reminds us of questions that have been raised frequently in the literature on school as community. Research has indicated consistently a much stronger sense of community in private schools than in public schools, because private school membership is voluntary and based on shared value systems (Bryk & Driscoll, 1988; Peshkin, 1995; Rowan, 1990). It is possible that public schools can never achieve the same level of sense of community. As Rowan (1990) states:

Communal forms of organization are more likely to be present in smaller schools, in schools that are ethnically homogeneous, and in schools that can control student entry and exit. To the extent that these conditions are lacking in many public schools, it should be more difficult for these schools to achieve communal organization. (p. 379)

The second discouraging lesson relates to the paradox of "going to scale" with models for community building. CPES is a product of individual initiative based on strongly held personal convictions. As Elmore (1996) points out, most innovative reforms in education emerge in this way, through the extraordinary energy of a few inspired educators, but seldom go to scale, or take hold, in the average school because of a variety of institutional and professional barriers. It is possible that community can never be created by systemic, comprehensive schemes (which are *gesellschaftlich*) but only through local initiative and dedication. How, then, can successful community-building initiatives ever go to scale and become the standard "metaphor" for American public schools?

Comer's School Development Program

Comer's School Development Program (SDP) focuses on at-risk students in urban elementary schools, emphasizing prevention over remediation. As we pointed out in Chapter 5, Comer's model includes a strong component of parent involvement as well as community building within the school. In this and other ways, it is similar to other comprehensive projects that focus on at-risk youth in urban settings (e.g., Levin's Accelerated Schools and Slavin's Success for All program; for comparisons among these programs and SDP, see King, 1994). Begun in 1968 in two public schools in New Haven, Connecticut, the SDP model is now in place in 563 schools in more than 80 districts in 21 states, and is being aggressively disseminated nationally through a system of regional centers (Comer et al., 1996).

The SDP model is based in Comer's synthesis of child development theory (Comer et al., 1996). He contends that there are six developmental "pathways" that are critical for academic learning—physical, cognitive, psychological, linguistic, social, and ethical—and that most public schools address only some of the pathways to the neglect of the others. To be effective, schools have to be "child-centered," that is, to address all six pathways. And to Comer, the child-centered school is synonymous with "community": "The SDP mechanisms are . . . essentially, a pathway toward community building" (p. 148).

Twenty-eight years of experience with implementing his ideas have led Comer and his colleagues to articulate a rather tidy model for the School Development Program consisting of three *mechanisms*, three guiding *principles*, and three primary *operations* to be implemented in each participating school. In what follows, we briefly describe the model, highlighting the features that are relevant to our analysis.

The three *mechanisms* are the School Planning and Management Team (SPMT), the Parent Team (PT), and the Student and Staff Support Team (SSST). The SPMT is the "central organizing body" of the school. Led by the principal, it includes teachers, parents, and support staff in its membership. The Parent Team consists, theoretically, of all parents of attending children. However, parent involvement is differentiated into three levels. At the first level, 50–100% of parents participate in the traditional activities of parent-teacher conferences and school social programs; at the second level, 10–50% of parents volunteer in the school to support its program; and, at the third level, 1–10% are representatives elected by the PT to be members of the SPMT (Comer et al., 1996). The third mechanism, the SSST, is similar to a traditional child study or multidisciplinary team. It consists of staff with child development and mental health knowledge and focuses on schoolwide "climate" and the needs of individual referred children.

In governing the school, these three *mechanisms* are responsible for three *operations*: Developing the Comprehensive School Plan, ensuring staff development, and assessing programs and outcomes. In performing these operations, all teams are to operate by three *principles*: collaboration, consensus, and "no-fault." The latter means that blaming—attributing failure to others—is avoided.

Comer's model is not particularly prescriptive as to curriculum and instruction to be adopted in SDP schools (King, 1994). However, the model strongly emphasizes measurable academic achievement, with standardized test scores as the criterion. Comer and his colleagues (1996) state their rationale for this focus:

> To be fair to students, we think the school's curriculum should be designed and implemented to ensure that they do well on standardized tests. . . . Standardized test results receive wide publicity, and the public judges schools particularly on the results of these tests. Given the importance of these tests to students' futures and the public at large, improving standardized test scores remains a primary target. (p. 99)

To help schools improve standardized test scores, the program draws on some traditional areas of school-effectiveness research, particularly academic learning time and curriculum alignment.

Evaluation and assessment are important foci in Comer's model, making it unusual in the reform movement. The project's multi-method assessment plan has demonstrated "significant student gains in achievement, attendance, behavior, and overall adjustment in SDP schools when compared to students in matched schools" (Comer et al., 1996, p. 20) and significant positive change in school climate.

Comer and his colleagues (1996) frequently use "community" as a metaphor for the SDP school, and many features of the model seem to reflect concerns with *gemeinschaftlich* qualities in schools: the focus on collaboration and consensus, the focus on the needs of the whole child, and the recognition of the "centrality of the family" to students' school success. However, taken as a whole, the SDP model has a *gesellschaftlich* feel to it, and the references to community seem somewhat rhetorical. First, although Comer and colleagues (1996) speak of transforming the school's "mission," the main objective in an SDP school is quite traditional—to raise achievement test scores. In our view, this unquestioning acceptance of the standardized test criterion for effectiveness reflects acceptance of the pervasive *gesellschaftlich* value of "productivity" in education and how to measure it. Rather than changing the *Gesellschaft* mission of the school, this acceptance would seem to reinforce it, to give it credibility. This is especially curious in a program aimed at inner-city, at-risk youth; many would argue that such youth have been disadvantaged by the biases inherent in standardized testing systems.

A second point, related to the first, is that SDP reflects few core changes in the hierarchical school structure. The principal continues in a traditional role, sharing decision making with a team; this configuration for SBM, as discussed in Chapter 5, has little impact on traditional influence relationships. And, since the goal of the school's program is given (to raise test scores), the mechanisms for parent involvement seem to reflect the "school-to-home" transmission model we examined in the last chapter, that is, their purpose is to get parent "buy-in" to the school-determined goals and program.

At this point, if we compared SDP with the Central Park East Schools, the similarities would be a strong "theory" to serve as the basis for shared values and a concern for students' academic success. The differences are several. SDP is meant to be implemented in schools of traditional size, while CPES emphasizes small size as a necessary condition for community building. SDP relies on formal mechanisms for parent involvement, determined by the school, rather than on informal collaboration between teachers and parents as seen in CPES. SDP's curriculum is traditional, determined by alignment with standardized tests, while CPES's is a "progressive" program developed by the teachers. And SDP is meant to be implemented in regular public schools, while Central Park East Schools are "alternative" schools of choice. It is likely that these differences impact the nature of community that can be created in the school. It is possible that the positive outcomes attributed to Comer's SDP are related as much to improvements made within the traditional schooling model in previously "failing" schools as to enhancing aspects of community.

Finally, both the SDP and CPES models grew from the initiative of dedicated individuals with strongly held convictions about reforming inner-city schools. CPES remains an informal, small-school model, while Comer's SDP has become an elaborate model that is being more widely disseminated. In our view, CPES has been more successful in creating community in schools. We begin to see some lessons here about going to scale with community reforms, and will return to this point in the chapter summary.

Sergiovanni's Proposal for Creating Community in Schools

How are schools to be reshaped as communities? Sergiovanni confronts this question in *Building Community in Schools* (1994) and provides the most prescriptive "handbook" available on this topic. Sergiovanni's theoretical perspective, like ours, is drawn from Tönnies's (1887/1957) theory of *Gemeinschaft* and *Gesellschaft*, and he applies the framework to argue that schools have been too "solidly ensconced in the *gesellschaft* camp" and need to move to the *Gemeinschaft* "side of the ledger" (p. 14). Commensurate with the qualities of *Gemeinschaft*, Sergiovanni defines community as "collections of individuals who are bonded together by natural will and [commitment] to a set of shared ideas and ideals" (p. xvi). He further sees communities in the *gemeinschaftlich* model as family-like, characterized by the emotions of "personalization, authenticity, caring and unconditional acceptance" (p. xvi).

Sergiovanni (1994) offers several ideas for building this type of community in schools. Two of his key ideas are to create a "community of mind" for educators and then to create a school program that is consonant with this community of mind. To become a community of mind, the school should identify and commit to a set of "core values" regarding "what schools are for, what is good for students . . . and how everyone involved should live their lives together" (p. 86). The set of core values can then be transformed into curricular decisions by developing an educational "platform" for the school. The platform is an agreement among teachers as to their aims for education, what students should achieve each year, preferred instructional methods, and so on. The shared platform is, then, a way to operationalize the school's community of mind.

Sergiovanni (1994) further suggests that to foster *gemeinschaftlich* relationships, classrooms should operate as "democratic communities" in which students share the responsibility for regulating their own and others' behavior. Students should be taught negotiating and moral reasoning to do this. Sergiovanni argues that *gesellschaftlich* discipline strategies of punishment and reward do not help students develop self-esteem and caring relationships with others. This notion of democratic classrooms is in the tradition of Dewey (1902) and Noddings (1992) in the belief that schools play a role in shaping society by teaching students to be "caring" citizens.

Finally, Sergiovanni (1994), similar to McLaughlin (1993) and others, urges that school staffs redefine colleagueship in order to evolve into a professional community. In a professional community of teachers, members strive toward a professional ideal made up of a commitment to exemplary practice and an ethic of caring. Sergiovanni's ideal of professional community emphasizes "virtue" as well as competence, and friendship ties among the members of the community.

Across all these areas of discussion, Sergiovanni (1994) returns to three central themes: (1) To create community in schools, educators must form a community of mind; (2) the "underlying theory of school itself" (p. 32) should be changed by moving from the metaphor of organization to the metaphor of community as the image for schools; and (3) relationships in schools should reflect the "natural will" of *Gemeinschaft*, that is, adults should be involved in a caring way in the lives of the students they serve. In sum, to Sergiovanni, creating community in schools involves educators' proactively creating the qualities of a community of mind within the existing school structure.

In approaching a critique of Sergiovanni's (1994) ideas, we note the strong theoretical perspective he brings to his analysis and recommendations. He fruitfully draws from Tönnies's (1887/1957) theory to sketch the current *gesellschaftlich* climate of most schools and to create a portrait of a *gemeinschaftlich* alternative—a community of mind based in caring and democratic natural-will relationships. In our view, this work is theoretically informed, extends the dialogue around community and education, and aims to make a difference in practice. However, it is also limited and perhaps misleading in terms of a deeper analysis of the community issue in schools and solutions proposed.

First, Sergiovanni's (1994) call for educators to create a community of mind stretches the definition of this concept. In our read of Toñnies (1887/1957), a community of mind is essentially a gathered community of individuals who are like-minded, who share fundamental values about how to live their lives. These individuals seek each other out for the intrinsic satisfaction of being together. Because being together is valued, a natural-will community of belongingness and trust is formed. Many churches illustrate this type of community in our contemporary society. In contrast, educators gather in schools primarily for career reasons—to make a living. They represent a wide range of life-styles, moral systems, and religious backgrounds. Their time and place of gathering, and many aspects of their working relationships, are "contractual." *After* they are gathered, they may indeed discover among themselves, or work to develop, shared educational values. But such a professional community of mind is always limited. It cannot create the same level of *gemeinschaftlich* experiences as a community of mind formed around fundamental values of life-style and morality. Thus, Sergiovanni's proposal to create community of mind in schools stretches the definition of this type of community, as defined by Tönnies, and may create expectations for *gemeinschaftlich* experiences of trust and unconditional belongingness that cannot be met. A more realistic concept for community of mind in schools might include the ideas of autonomy and choice forwarded by Battistich and colleagues (1995) discussed earlier. In our view, these amendments to the community concept more accurately capture the realities of modern life and make it clearer that there are limits on the type of community of mind and "belongingness" that can be achieved in schools.

Second, Sergiovanni (1994) seems to consider the school a closed system and to ignore the interface between the school and the surrounding community. In his proposal, educators are in the spotlight as they are urged to form communities of mind among themselves and to foster natural-will relationships with students. We think that focusing on educators alone as the creators of school community is misguided on two counts. First, it will only perpetuate the problem of the disconnect between the values of the school and the values of the subcommunities served by the school, a major factor in the alienation between school and community. Second, a school is a community only if belongingness is promoted for students as well as faculty. While Sergiovanni certainly addresses this need, particularly in discussing teachers' responsibility to create caring, democratic classrooms, it should not be assumed that educators' values alone can create community in which students can feel comfortable, in which they "belong." It is necessary for students to know that their families' values are respected in the

school and reflected in its program. Here, we would contrast Sergiovanni's ideas with the approach in the Central Park East Schools, in
which respect for parents' values is proactively addressed in order to
build an environment of trust for students.

   Third, while educators may be able to make progress in adopting a
new "metaphor" for schools, changing the "theory" does not change the
reality of how schools are structured and governed. In other words,
simply *thinking* of schools differently, as communities rather than
as organizations, does not alter the deep structures of the school as
organization, structures that are institutionalized and that help create
the *gesellschaftlich* climate of schools. Here we think that Sergiovanni
(1994) simply does not go deep enough into the issues, in particular,
the bureaucratic, hierarchical structure and the size of schools as organizations. Again, we would compare Sergiovanni's proposals with
the CPES model, which attended to both the hierarchical structure and
size issues.

THE PROMISE OF COMMUNITY-BUILDING REFORMS

What can be expected from these proposals to create community in
schools? What is their promise? In addressing these questions, it is
important to keep in mind that there is a very limited research base on
creating community in schools, though there is some research that
links community-type qualities to effectiveness, as we have discussed,
and some research demonstrating that students do well in some of the
models we have examined here, such as Comer et al.'s (1996) model
and the Central Park East Schools. Further, most of the models and
ideas for creating community here have not yet been widely implemented and evaluated. While Comer's model is being implemented in
a growing number of schools, it is difficult at this point to evaluate the
faithfulness to the original SDP model in this wider dissemination.
And to our knowledge Sergiovanni's rather prescriptive ideas for creating community have not been systematically implemented and evaluated. Our consideration of the promise of these ideas is, then, at a
speculative analytical level.

   Based on our earlier analysis of the drift to *Gesellschaft* (see Chapter 4), our first concern is whether these proposals have any impact on
the hierarchical, centralized school structure, which we have identified as a barrier to the experience of community in schools. From the
models we sampled, we see a varied picture here. Sergiovanni (1994)
does not attend explicitly to this issue, while Comer's model (Comer

et al., 1996) calls for some changes in decision making but leaves the traditional hierarchical structure intact. In fact, Comer's model involves some elaboration of the bureaucratic structure with the establishment of formal "mechanisms" for governance (i.e., the SPMT, PT, and SSST). Meier's (1995) model at CPES appears to alter the structure by creating a "staff-run" school, but only at the individual, small-school level. Our conclusion is that the school-as-community movement as represented in these samples pays attention only superficially to the issue of bureaucratic structure and how this has worked to damage community in school. Often, the assumption appears to be that community-type qualities can simply be imported into individual schools and classrooms without attending at all to the bureaucratic structure of the school and school district.

Our second concern is that contemporary schools reflect an embedded *Gesellschaft* "mission" that is a barrier to community. We think that proposals to create a community of mind among educators do not take this factor sufficiently into account. Such proposals assume that there is sort of a vacuum existing around the school's mission and that educators in individual schools might be free to recreate their own sense of mission. In reality, the educational system is pervaded with *gesellschaftlich* values of economic competitiveness and metaphors of productivity, which are continually reiterated in federal and state educational policies and testing programs. We believe that educators attempts to identify shared core values can have only limited results unless the *major* issue of the pervasiveness of *gesellschaftlich* values is addressed. To do this, the very heart of the school's program—what is taught and why—must be reexamined. In our sampling here, Sergiovanni (1994) ignores the broader issue and simply assumes that educators within the individual school can articulate their own "platform," while Comer et al. (1996) in fact reinforce the *Gesellschaft* mission with SDP's emphasis on achievement tests. Meier (1995), in the Central Park East Schools, does appear to move to a new mission around respect for both the power of students' ideas and their families' values, and progressive educational practices. Again, however, Meier's model was developed in a small alternative school.

Our third concern centers on the interface between the school and the surrounding community. Some proposals to reshape the school as a community appear to consider the school a closed system. These proposals often focus on what the professionals *within* the school think and do to promote community qualities, ignoring the connection between the school *as* community and the community beyond the school. Other proposals attempt to link with the community as represented only by parents of the children in the school. Here, Comer et al. (1996) try to get parents involved in supporting the school-defined program through formal mechanisms of shared decision making, while the Central Park East Schools focus on informal, collaborative relationships between parents and teachers to build trust. We think the informal, personalized connections between school and parents emphasized by CPES, which are made possible by the school's small size, hold the most promise across the examined models. However, none of the community-building proposals we have reviewed make strong attempts to link the school with other community members besides parents, as far as we can determine.

A fourth concern focuses on the paradox of going to scale with community proposals. It appears to us that more elaborate models for community building that are intended to be disseminated (like Comer's) have less success in producing *gemeinschaftlich* qualities in schools because they are too formal, too bureaucratic—in fact, too *gesellschaftlich*. From our sampling, it appears that small-scale, informal approaches (e.g., CPES) hold the most promise. Thus, it may be that re-creating community in American schools depends more on individual initiative in small schools at the local level than on grand, reproducible schemes.

In sum, we think that proposals to reshape schools as community hold some promise, but are limited. While rightly aimed at inspiring educators to confront the *gesellschaftlich* qualities of schools and demonstrating that some *gemeinschaftlich* qualities can be recovered, they tend to avoid the deeper, problematic issues related to the school's mission and school-community connections. Their remedies do not go deep enough. In the case of Sergiovanni's (1994) proposals, for example, simply *thinking* differently by adopting a different metaphor doesn't get at the fundamental reasons for the drift to *Gesellschaft* in the first place. Further, proposals to create community in schools may present us with false promises. It is possible that the type of community that can be created in schools is limited and that it can be created only by like-minded people who have the rare opportunity to gather together around shared values, as in Central Park East Schools, and can never "go to scale."

7

Paradox and Promise

Home is where we start from. As one grows older
The world becomes stranger, the patterns more complicated
　　　　　　　— *T. S. Eliot* The Four Quartets, East Coker

In this book we have attempted to understand why, despite heroic and expensive reform efforts, we seem to experience less and less satisfaction with community in our schools today. We have examined the issues of community in schools through the lens of classic *Gemeinschaft/Gesellschaft* theory with a mind toward more contemporary views of community. We have undertaken these efforts because we are strong advocates of community; we believe that schools have become too *gesellschaftlich*. But we also see a problem with most of the community reforms — that they are generally atheoretical. We have offered a theory of community that we hope will lead to reforms that are more sound and have a greater chance of success. We do not want to see American schools abandon attempts at community as another disappointing fad because they were based on naive notions of community or shallow implications for practice.

　　Based on the discussion in the preceding chapters, it is clear that we must live simultaneously in *Gemeinschaft* and *Gesellchaft*. Good school people have long intuitively felt the bind to be both more organized and more personalized. The analysis that we have presented here recognizes that these characteristics have certain polar pulls such that as we increase one characteristic we may be decreasing the other. As we try to bring organization to a school, we are probably causing it to become less intimate, and as we increase proximity and intimacy, we reduce the uniformity and efficiency of our organization.

　　In the title of this chapter, we have purposefully reversed the terms *paradox* and *promise* from our original order in the title because the dilemmas embedded in the community movement have come to the forefront in our analysis. But these reforms also hint at some promises. In this chapter we summarize the paradoxes within these reform efforts, as well as these promises. We conclude by considering realistic directions for community and schools based on what we have learned from our analysis. In this way we hope to be able to avert the inevitable disappointment and disillusionment of the paradoxes we have discussed. We offer a theoretical perspective, not a solution; we believe that we have found some promising aspects to the reforms we have examined, but much work needs to be done yet in creating models of effective school-community.

THE PROBLEMS AND PARADOX
OF COMMUNITY REFORMS

We have examined several groups of reforms that attempt to create community within schools or enhance school-community connections. We have analyzed the reforms by considering whether they address the underlying issues of community and the drift toward *Gesellschaft*. We think that most of these reforms involve bureaucratic solutions; they tinker around the margins of the problem and are based on naive notions of community. Unwittingly, they create tensions that will ultimately prevent them from succeeding. We have grouped these problems and paradoxes into four categories, which we will address one by one.

Attempting to Achieve That Which Cannot Be

Reforms are generally not built on a realistic notion of community; they rarely address the complexities and characteristics of modern life. Schools no longer connect with one, homogeneous, stable neighborhood. They must accommodate the mobility of modern life and the modern demands for choice. Families move frequently and most expect their children to be able to live and work in communities other than the ones in which they were born. Parents want to be able to enroll their children in schools near work locations or child-care facilities that may be some distance from where they live. Children need opportunities to learn beyond the idiosyncracies of an isolated community. Parents today have many demands on their time and energy; there are few parents who can give long periods of time to their children's schools. Reforms that require a lot of parent involvement are difficult to maintain.

Many reforms have failed because their creators do not realize that some centralized control is inevitable. Not all communities have the same power and wealth. Paradoxically, modern notions of justice have weakened the ties between schools and neighborhoods by demanding that we equalize educational opportunities for children regardless of the wealth of their family or community. With equalized funding come increased regulations and expectations, and this has led to the imposition of accountability measures across district lines: We must assure various governing bodies that students have learned, and we must assure the public that their money has been spent wisely. We inevitably do these things through standardized means—tests and audits, means of assuring uniformity. Most attempts at school-level management remove curricular dictates, but impose some form of testing, with the message "we don't care what methods you use, that is up to local teachers—*as long as the job gets done.*" Reformers seldom realize that these accountability measures are as controlling to local schools as the previously dictated methods, which they give up with such fanfare. Today we cannot give up all forms of centralized accountability. Even advocates of decentralization, as in Chicago (Applebome, 1995), have recognized that a certain amount of central oversight is necessary.

Teachers, parents, and children all live in many communities simultaneously. People do not live or work in cohesive, homogeneous groups today. Because we place a high value on choice, schools must accommodate mobility. Many reforms have attempted to emphasize a few aspects of community without acknowledging that the community must compete with other connections in people's lives or the deeper issues that divide us. The most obvious examples are the attempt to create a "professional community" from a disparate group of teachers, as discussed in Johnson (1990) and McLaughlin (1993), or the attempt to teach a set of moral standards without addressing the difference in deeply held values as in Boyer's Basic School (1995). While the groups formed have a certain amount of cohesion and a certain set of unifying values, because they fail to acknowledge the differences and deep divisions, they expect the same kind of security and identity that would have resulted from a much more *gemeinschaftlich* group. Groups of this kind, with values and similarities defined but limited, can function well. They can accomplish tasks and work to mutual advantage—they are good for schools; they just cannot deliver the profound sense of belonging, identity, and security of *Gemeinschaft* of kinship or place. For these reasons, Young (1986) abandoned the word *community* in favor of "social relationships of unassimilated otherness" (p. 23), and Battistich and colleagues (1995) modified their definition of community to emphasize inclusivity, equality, and participation.

Applying Bureaucratic Solutions to Problems of Community

A second major paradox is created by attempting to build community through bureaucratic means. We try to create schools that are intimate, caring, and personalized. In doing this we must recognize that there is no "technology of *Gemeinschaft*." When we create strategies, job descriptions, and task forces we are not operating in a manner consistent with *Gemeinschaft*; when we are *gemeinschaftlich* we operate in what has been called "folkways" (Redfield, 1955). Our bureaucratic mind set has convinced us that the only way to get something done in the schools is to set a goal, develop a strategy, create a special function with a budget and a person in charge. In other words, we routinely and indiscriminately seek bureaucratic solutions to our problems, even problems of community.

Many new techniques in schools attempt to provide an atmosphere in which students feel secure both physically and psychologically. They often try to improve schools' ability to provide the social monitoring and care that children got naturally in a *Gemeinschaft*. In Chapter 5 we gave an example of school reform—coordination of children's services—in which reformers tried to simplify services to community clients, but in doing so elaborated the school bureaucracy.

So today, some of our goals focus on trying to restore and re-create qualities that schools had in simpler days, making our schools more personal. But the habits of bureaucratic behavior are so fully developed that it is the only way we know how to behave in organization. We have lost the ability to identify and use the techniques of folkways. Folkways have become low-tech and too old fashioned. We think of them as ways of circumventing the bureaucracy, not legitimate ways of behaving in the workplace.

Failing to Challenge the Increasingly
Gesellschaftlich Mission of Schools

One of the strongest points throughout our analysis of programs was the pervasiveness of the *gesellschaftlich* mission in American schools. The thorniest problems are created because educators rarely recognize or confront this issue. Schools always have and probably always will serve to educate children to be "productive citizens." What does this mean when the traditional ideals of democracy have been overshadowed by the ideals of efficiency and uniform standards? Educators must recognize the overwhelming character of *Gesellschaft* in order to deal with it and its implications. They have to confront the conflict created between a highly structured bureaucracy and the ideal of democratic participation. School people must examine their role in this conflict. Perhaps it is time to begin creating a new mission for the schools in which they teach and model to children authentic ways to participate in multicultural democracy. Educators must examine the pervasiveness of the corporate mind set in education, which is, in the theory we have presented, antithetical to this goal. Despite decades of talk about decentralization and school-level management, schools are becoming increasingly centralized, complex, and specialized. Schools are asked to be efficient and maintain uniform standards. Business calls for schools to prepare better workers. The courts have asked schools to meet the needs of various groups of students. All these expectations require organization and bureaucracy, which in our analysis reduces the ability to build community.

None of the reforms we have examined has really succeeded in shifting control of the school from the groups that have long held power. Even in the Chicago attempt to decentralize school governance, school personnel have made most of the decisions about the school program and those parents who were involved to any extent were the few who have always been active in schools. Most reforms, such as interagency collaboration and home-school partnerships, retain the strongly *gesellschaftlich* notion of the school's professional expertise bringing services to clients. It is very hard to see the school personnel as agents of the people they serve.

The Paradox of Systemic Reform

One of the most perplexing paradoxes we see is what is sometimes called "systemic reform." Most reformers apply the term to a pervasive reform that changes the institution of the school at all levels. But systemic reform can have two meanings. First, it can mean that which is characteristic of a system, connoting orderliness, predictability, and uniformity. Second, it can mean growing organically and naturally from some internal impetus within the system. These two definitions can be quite contradictory in our analysis. The hope of most reformers is that a systemic reform, being pervasive and deep, will generalize well to new sites, and become the way in which most schools operate. While most school people want to develop a reform that generalizes well, very few have succeeded. The paradox seems to be that systemic reform in the organic sense can never be translated into systemic reform in the "highly organized" sense.

The school reforms we have examined attempt to establish community by working on one or two aspects, but they are doomed to limited results if they don't consider both internal and external relationships. We have criticized Sergiovani (1994) for working as if the school were a closed system. The same criticism could be raised in most of the school-as-community reforms. Unless these reforms take into account the external aspects of the lives of the people in the school, the school simply becomes a bunker in a hostile or impersonal world.

Comer et al.'s reforms (1996) seem to be the most complete, dealing with both internal and external aspects of community, but these reforms are a bit too pat or heirachical, in retaining the *Gesellschaft* notion of professional expertise. It seems that once reformers attempt to bring all the pieces into alignment, the reform becomes rigid and loses the responsiveness that was its intent.

There are really two issues within this paradox: whether a reform deals with both internal and external aspects of community, and whether it can be generalized to other settings. Both issues tempt us with solutions of bringing all aspects of the reform into alignment and setting standards by which it will operate. We generally are unable to stop short of turning the reform into another bureaucracy. It appears that this paradox is seen most clearly through the analysis of *Gemeinschaft* and *Gesellschaft*. We may reach the unavoidable conclusion that *Gemeinschaft* simply cannot "go to scale." This may be one of the keys to understanding why these reforms have been lauded for their idiosyncratic success, but criticized for their failure to transfer to other sites or to achieve large-scale changes.

THE PROMISE OF COMMUNITY REFORM

From the analysis in this book, an image begins to emerge of how a school might look that has both a robust internal community and strong, responsive connections to the external community. While no one reform we have examined embodies all that we hope, many offer pieces that contribute to what we envision. In this section we look at these pieces.

Small Schools

It would appear that at least for younger children, there are few good substitutes for the small neighborhood school. Despite the possible lack of racial or ethnic diversity, parents want their young children near them. Flexible boundaries and some enrollment choice permitting children to attend school near a parent's workplace seems to satisfy most of the demands families express beyond the neighborhood school.

The work of Meier (1995) and the Central Park East Schools would indicate that small schools may be best for older students as well. These schools and others that have grown out of Sizer's (1984) Essential Schools illustrate that longer contact with fewer teachers, and a narrower range of curricular offerings, reduces the anonymity for high school students as well as young children.

Small schools, small classes seem to offer more personalization than do elaborate specialized programs. A good teacher with a small group of students can accomplish a great deal. Noddings (1992), Boyer (1995), and Meier (1995) have all suggested that prolonged periods of time with one teacher, narrowing the range of contacts, builds stability and personalized relationships. Educators must have the courage to resist the lure of continuing to add more and more specialized programs and ask whether giving childen specialized assistance, in or out of the classroom, is worth the social cost. Increased specialist services lead to fragmented days and complicated schedules, threatening the intimacy and integrity of the classroom group. Some schools have begun to ask what would happen if all special funds were used to hire more classroom teachers so as to create smaller classes.

Informality and Trust

Above all, small schools seem to operate in informal ways and develop stronger bonds of trust. Students are known individually, and, with fewer external subcommunities, it is easier to be responsive to students' families. Perhaps the most promising reform we have examined in this book is Debra Meier's Central Park East Schools (1995). These reforms have been built on relationships both inside and outside the school because Meier believes that students can develop a sense of belonging only in schools that their parents trust. Yet she has not established *formal* systems of parental participation and control, choosing to operate by what we have called "folkways." Her reform is "systemic" clearly in the second, "organic," sense. She builds trust through familiarity, which is possible in a small class and a small school, rather than building trust through the predictability of a system. Meier's emphasis on trust hearkens back to Fukuyama's work (1995), in which he says that our highly individualistic world leads people to be suspicious of each other, eroding our social capital. He suggests that working in small groups on issues of mutual importance leads us to trust those in our society.

Changing the Metaphor of School

If we are ever going to change the underlying *gesellschaftlich* mission of the school, we must think about schools in different ways. Those writers who suggest changing the metaphor for schooling may be closest to this. Both McLaughlin (1993) and Sergiovanni (1994) have suggested that "community" rather than "organization" should be the metaphor for schools. Beck (1994) suggests that leaders who think of governance in a new way would take a circle as a model instead of a pyramid, implying a whole new set of relationships. While school people are often frustrated by the lack of definition in changing a metaphor and often prefer a highly presciptive reform agenda, it is probably the case that we have never really conceptualized the schools in a new way and that reforms have become simply the substitution of one bureaucracy for another.

Meaningful Local Involvement in School Governance

People need a voice in local schools. Local site teams that remain strongly controlled by a centralized board wield very little power. At best, they are often seen as conduits to take the schools' message back to external constituencies. Educators have to develop ways of hearing their local communities and involving them in authentic ways in schools. Site councils will have little impact on the overall nature of the school if the *gesellschaftlich* values of the central board continue to dominate school district policy.

So far reforms in school governance seem to offer little promise. Chicago's decentralization has become mired in its own brand of bureaucracy and cynicism. Comer et al.'s (1996) use of parent committees seems to be one of the most promising, but also runs the risk of becoming bureaucratic. As the site-based movement matures, educators and policymakers must consider how to restructure the governance of local school districts. It may be possible to devolve critical policy decisions regarding the instructional program to local site councils with the school district organization serving a management function.

Ultimately we must ask programs that claim to have instituted community governance of schools to what extent the school program is open to negotiation with the community. Both Chicago and Comer's schools seem to fail this test. Curriculum remains highly centralized in Chicago, and Comer's main measure of achievement is standardized tests.

MOVING AHEAD: LEARNING TO LIVE WITH PARADOX

Today we must recognize that schools are a mix of *Gemeinschaft* and *Gesellschaft*. In addition to these simultaneous and conflicting demands, there is an increasing awareness that schools may be one of the few social institutions left that bridge the gap between the individual or family and the larger civic society. Citizens need to voice their values and preferences as a means of shaping society. Where in the past a number of voluntary social organizations allowed people to work together to build a network of social capital, these groups are diminishing rapidly, and people are asking the state or large social service agencies to provide general community services (Elshtain, 1995; Fukuyama, 1995; Putnam, 1995; Sandel, 1996). Thus a school system that allows for sufficient exchange with the public may be a key factor in maintaining a democracy in the United States. It may give Americans the hope they need to maintain their participation in the larger society; it may give us all the arena we need in which to work out ways to live among people who are different from us.

Sandal (1996) points out that civic behavior has always been rooted in small, bounded places and that today we live in a multiplicity of settings, from neighborhoods, to nations, to the world as a whole. This requires citizens who can abide the ambiguity associated with divided affiliations. From this it follows that the mission of the school must be:

- To teach students to live satisfying lives as participants in groups at various levels
- To learn to live and work in groups in which differences are accepted and respected
- To learn to form groups that provide satisfaction, identity, and security without destroying choices and opportunities for others

This mission is not very different from that which has been espoused for many years by Dewey (1938/1963) and his followers. The curriculum of a school with this new mission must be looked at in light of the work of critical theorists such as Giroux (1992a, b), who have clearly seen that democratic aspects of schooling become overshadowed by the *gesellschaftlich* focus on economic competitiveness.

Greene (1993) has shown ways in which the curriculum can be broadened to include learning about others in ways that respect differences and enrich the larger group.

If schools are to be more *gemeinschaftlich*, there will be certain implications for the way they operate. *Gemeinschaft* requires constancy, intimacy, time, proximity, and commitment. This kind of commonality can come about through a number of ways, and Friedman (1982) reminds us that it is most effective when it is "discovered" in a preexisting, natural condition. *Gemeinschaft* can be created by choice, but for schools to do so requires giving up some choices and tolerating some idiosyncratic procedures and outcomes. Above all, it will mean releasing some of the control of schooling that professionals have jealously guarded for so long and learning to think of the school as an agency of the citizenry.

We must be realistic and give up our nostalgic, small-town fetish and our sentimental attachments to an idealized version of community. The demands of the modern world require some centralized control, some uniformity from site to site, and some specialization. We cannot operate today without some *gesellschaftlich* qualities in our schools. We must acquire a new, balanced set of skills, which have been developed to meet both sets of needs, and which must be used judiciously and carefully, recognizing that employing one set of skills naturally imposes a certain limit on the other. We can't have a life or a school that is only *Gemeinschaft* today; modern society simply will not tolerate it. Neither can we have a life or a school that is only *Gesellschaft*, because human nature will not tolerate it.

In order to avoid the dependence on *gesellschaftlich* techniques, we must develop a comparable repertoire of behavior consistent with *Gemeinschaft*. Retaining and making legitimate the informal behavior that has served us well in the past may be the greatest challenge for the future. To allow ourselves to use informal means to solve problems, to allow small groups of people to seek and develop their own goals and means within very broad organizational limits, will be difficult.

We would offer an example of a modern writer who dignifies folkways as being appropriate for organizations. James March, who has always seen rational behavior to be severely limiting for organizations (1988), was quoted recently as saying that efficiency was an inappropriate goal for higher education (O'Toole, 1995). Efficiency has long been considered the ultimate goal of modern management, and only someone of March's stature could suggest that it should not be our goal. We no doubt have many other folkways available to us; perhaps we should think carefully about them and give ourselves permission to use them.

CONCLUSION

We believe that our schools can contribute more to our larger communities and can be better communities in themselves. This requires careful thought about what community means today. We need continued experimentation with small schools and intimate settings. We need more people who are willing to challenge the myth of going to scale and who see the goodness in something unique and small. Educators should think carefully about what they undertake in reforming our schools. It is wrong to ask the public to participate in reform movements that are doomed because of underlying inconsistencies. It is too easy today for the public to be cynical about our schools. We need legitimate and thoughtful work to build better communities. We do not need paradox disguised as promise.

References

Alexander, L. (1993). School choice in the year 2000. *Phi Delta Kappan, 74*(10), 762–766.

Applebome, P. (1995, November 8). Chicago experiment offers lessons, but not verdict on decentralization. *The New York Times*, p. B6.

Arvey, H. H., & Tijerina, A. (1995). The school of the future: Implementation issues in a school-community connection. In L. C. Rigsby, M. C. Reynolds, M. C. Wang (Eds.), *School-community connections: Exploring issues for research and practice* (pp. 311–355). San Francisco: Jossey-Bass.

Bacharach, S. B. (Ed.). (1990). *Education reform: Making sense of it all*. Boston: Allyn and Bacon.

Battistich, V., Solomon, D., Kim, D., Watson, M., & Schaps, E. (1995). Schools as communities, poverty levels of student populations, and students' attitudes, motives, and performance: A multilevel analysis. *American Educational Research Journal, 32*, 627–658.

Beck, L. (1994). *Reclaiming educational administration as a caring profession*. New York: Teachers College Press.

Bellah, R. (1985). *Habits of the heart*. Berkeley: University of California Press.

Bender, T. (1978). *Community and social change in America*. New Brunswick, NJ: Rutgers University Press.

Blackledge, A. (1995). Minority parents as school governors in Chicago and Britain: Empowerment or not? *Educational Review, 47*, 309–317.

Blau, P. (1974). *On the nature of oranizations*. New York: John Wiley & Sons.

Blau, P. M., & Scott, W. R. (1962). *Formal organizations*. San Francisco: Chandler.

Boyer, E. (1983). *High school: A report on secondary education in America*. New York: Harper & Row.

Boyer, E. (1987). *College: The undergraduate experience in America*. New York: Harper & Row.

Boyer, E. (1991). *Ready to learn: A mandate for the nation*. Princeton, NJ: The Carnegie Foundation.

Boyer, E. (1995). *The basic school: A community for learning*. Princeton, NJ: The Carnegie Foundation.

Bridges, W. (1994). *Jobshift*. New York: Addison-Wesley.

Brophy, J. E., & Good, T. L. (1986). Teacher behavior and student achievement. In M. C. Wittrock (Ed.), *Handbook of research on teaching* (3rd ed., pp. 328–375). New York: Macmillan.

Brown, D. J. (1992). The recentralization of school districts. *Educational Policy, 6*, 289–297.

Bryk, A. (1988). Musings on the moral life of schools. *American Journal of Education, 96,* 256–290.

Bryk, A., & Driscoll, M. (1988). *The high school as community: Contextual influences and consequences for students and teachers.* Madison: Wisconsin Center for Education Research, University of Wisconsin–Madison.

Bryk, A. S., Easton, J. Q., Kerbow, D., Rollow, S. G., & Sebring, P. A. (1993). *A view from the elementary schools: The state of reform in Chicago.* Chicago: Consortium on Chicago School Research.

Callahan, R. E. (1962). *Education and the cult of efficiency.* Chicago: University of Chicago Press.

Clark, T. A. (1991). *Collaboration to build competence.* Washington, DC: U.S. Government Printing Office.

Coleman, J. S. (1985). Schools and the communities they serve. *Phi Delta Kappan, 66,* 527–532.

Coleman, J. S. (1987). Families and schools. *Educational Researcher, 16*(6), 32–38.

Comer, J. P. (1988). Educating poor children. *Scientific American, 259*(5), 42–48.

Comer, J. P., Haynes, N. M., Joyner, E. T., & Ben-Avie, M. (Eds.). (1996). *Rallying the whole village: The Comer process for reforming education.* New York: Teachers College Press.

Cremin, L. A. (1988). *American education: The metropolitan experience.* New York: Harper & Row.

Crowson, R. L. (1992). *School community relations, under reform.* Berkeley, CA: MuCutchan.

Crowson, R. L., & Boyd, W. L. (1993). Coordinating services for children: Designing arks for storms and seas unknown. *American Journal of Education, 101*(2), 140–179.

Crowson, R. L., & Boyd, W. L. (1995). Integration of services for children: A political economy of institutions perspective. In L. C. Rigsby, M. C. Reynolds, & M. C. Wang (Eds.), *School-community connections: Exploring issues for research and practice* (pp. 121–141). San Francisco: Jossey-Bass.

Crowson, R. L., & Boyd, W. L. (1996). The politics of education, the new institutionalism, and reinvented schooling: Some concluding observations. In R. L. Crowson, W. L. Boyd, & H. B. Mawhinney (Eds.), *The politics of education and the new institutionalism: Reinventing the American school* (pp. 203–214). Washington, DC: Falmer Press.

Cuban, L. (1988). A fundamental puzzle of school reform. *Phi Delta Kappan, 69*(5), 340–344.

Cuban, L. (1990). Reforming again, again, and again. *Educational Researcher, 19*(1), 3–13.

Cunningham, L. L. (1990). Educational leadership and administration: Retrospective and prospective views. In B. Mitchell & L. L. Cunningham (Eds.), *Educational leadership and changing contexts of families, communities, and schools: Eighty-ninth yearbook of the National Society for the Study of Education* (pp. 1–18). Chicago: University of Chicago Press.

Dewey, J. (1902). *The child and the curriculum.* Chicago: University of Chicago Press.

Dewey, J. (1927). *The public and its problems*. New York: Holt.

Dewey, J. (1963). *Experience and education*. New York: Collier Books. (Original work published 1938)

Dickens, C. (1989). *Hard times*. Oxford: Oxford University Press. (Original work published 1854)

Drucker, P. (1994, November). The age of social transformation. *The Atlantic Monthly, 275,* 53–80.

Dunkle, M. C. (1995). *Who controls major federal programs for childen & families: Rube Goldberg revisited* (Special Report 3). Washington, DC: Institute for Educational Leadership Policy Exchange.

Durkheim, E. (1951). *Suicide*. (J. Spaulding & G. Simpson, Trans.). Glencoe, IL: The Free Press. (Original work published 1897)

Durkheim, E. (1984). *The Division of labor in society* (W. D. Halls, Trans.). New York: Free Press. (Original work published 1893)

Eliot, T. S. (1943). *Four Quartets*. San Diego, CA: Harcourt Brace.

Elmore, R. F. (1991). Foreword. In G. A. Hess, Jr., *School restructuring, Chicago style* (pp. vii–ix). Newbury Park, CA: Corwin Press.

Elmore, R. F. (1996). Getting to scale with good educational practice. *Harvard Educational Review, 66*(1), 1–26.

Elshtain, J. (1982, April). Antigone's daughters. *Democracy, 2,* 46–59.

Elshtain, J. (1995). *Democracy on trial*. New York: Basic Books.

Epstein, J. (1995). School/family/community partnerships: Caring for the children we share. *Phi Delta Kappan, 76,* 701–712.

Etzioni, A. (1993). *The spirit of community*. New York: Touchstone.

First, P. F., Curcio, J. L., & Young, D. L. (1994). State full service school initiatives: New notions of policy development. In L. Adler & S. Gardner (Eds.), *The politics of linking schools and social services* (pp. 63–73). Washington, DC: The Falmer Press.

Fischer, C. (1982). *To dwell among friends*. Chicago: University of Chicago Press.

Friedman, M. (1982). Feminism and modern friendship: Dislocating the community. In C. Sunstein (Ed.), *Feminism and political theory* (pp. 143–158). Chicago: University of Chicago Press.

Fuhrman, S. H., Elmore, R. F., & Massell, D. (1993). School reform in the United States: Putting it into context. In S. L. Jacobson & R. Berne (Eds.), *Reforming education: The emerging systemic approach* (pp. 3–27). Thousand Oaks, CA: Corwin Press.

Fukuyama, F. (1995) *Trust*. New York: Free Press.

Furman, G. C., & Merz, C. (1996). Schools and community connections: Applying a sociological framework. In J. Cibulka & W. Kritek (Eds.), *Coordination among schools, families and communities: Prospects for educational reform* (pp. 323–347). Albany: State University of New York Press.

Gans, H. (1962). Urbanism and suburbanism as ways of life: A re-evaluation of definitions. In A. Rose (Ed.) *Human behavior and social processes: An interactionist approach* (pp. 70–85). Boston: Houghton Mifflin.

Gardner, S. (1990). Failure by fragmentation. *Equity and Choice, 6*(2), 4–12.

Gardner, S. (1994). Afterword. In L. Adler & S. Gardner (Eds.), *The politics of linking schools and social services* (pp. 189–199). Washington, DC: The Falmer Press.

Gilligan, C. (1982). *In a different voice.* Cambridge: Harvard University Press.

Giroux, H. A. (1992a). *Border crossings: Cultural workers and the politics of education.* New York: Routledge.

Giroux, H. (1992b). *Educational leadership and the crisis of democratic culture.* University Park, PA: University Council for Educational Administration.

Grant, G. (1988). *The world we created at Hamilton High.* Cambridge: Harvard University Press.

Gray, B. (1995). Obstacles to success in educational collaborations. In L. C. Rigsby, M. C. Reynolds, & M. C. Wang (Eds.), *School-community connections: Exploring issues for research and practice* (pp. 71–99). San Francisco: Jossey-Bass.

Greene, M. (1993). The passions of pluralism: Multiculturalism and the expanding community. *Educational Researcher, 22*(1), 13–18.

Halliger, P., & Murphy, J. (1986). The social context of effective schools. *American Journal of Education, 94,* 328–355.

Henry, M. (1996). *Parent-school collaboration: Feminist organizational structures and school leadership.* Albany: State University of New York Press.

Hess, G. A., Jr. (1991). *School restructuring, Chicago style.* Newbury Park, CA: Corwin Press.

Hess, G. A., Jr. (1995). *Restructuring urban schools: A Chicago perspective.* New York: Teachers College Press.

Himmelfarb, G. (1995). *The de-moralization of society.* New York: Alfred A. Knopf.

Hodgkinson, H. L. (1989). *The same client: The demographics of education and service delivery systems.* Washington, DC: Institute for Educational Leadership.

Hoffer, T., & Coleman, J. (1990). Changing families and communities: Implications for schools. In I. B. Mitchell & L. L. Cunningham (Eds.), *Educational leadership and the changing contexts of families, communities and schools: Eighty-ninth Yearbook of the National Society for the Study of Education* (pp. 118–134). Chicago: University of Chicago Press.

Hord, S. M. (1986). A synthesis of research on organizational collaboration. *Educational Leadership, 43*(5), 22–26.

Hoyt, K. (1991). Education reform and relationships between the private sector and education: A call for integration. *Phi Delta Kappan, 72,* 450–453.

Jackson, P. (1968). *Life in classrooms.* New York: Holt, Rinehart & Winston.

Jacobson, S. L., & Berne, R. (1993). (Eds.). *Reforming education: The emerging systemic approach.* Thousand Oaks, CA: Corwin Press.

Johnson, S. M. (1990). *Teachers at Work.* New York: Basic Books.

King, J. A. (1994). Meeting the educational needs of at-risk students: A cost analysis of three models. *Education Evaluation and Policy Analysis, 16,* 1–19.

Kirst, M. W. (1990). The crash of the first wave. In S. B. Bacharach (Ed.), *Education reform: Making sense of it all* (pp. 20-29). Boston: Allyn and Bacon.

Kirst, M. W. (1991). Improving children's services: Overcoming barriers, creating new opportunities. *Phi Delta Kappan, 73,* 615-618.

Kirst, M. W., & McLaughlin, M. (1990). Rethinking policy for children: Implications for educational administration. In B. Mitchell & L. L. Cunningham (Eds.), *Educational leadership and changing contexts of families, communities, and schools: Eighty-ninth yearbook of the National Society for the Study of Education* (pp. 69-90). Chicago: University of Chicago Press.

Knapp, M. S. (1995). How shall we study comprehensive, collaborative services for children and families? *Educational Researcher, 24*(4), 5-16.

Knapp, M. S., Barnard, K., Brandon, R. N., Gehrke, N. J., Smith, A. J., & Teather, E. C. (1994). University-based preparation for collaborative interprofessional practice. In L. Adler & S. Gardner (Eds.), *The politics of linking schools and social services* (pp. 137-151). Washington, DC: The Falmer Press.

Lewis, D. A. (1993). Deinstitutionalization and school decentralization: Making the same mistake twice. In J. Hannaway & M. Carnoy (Eds.), *Decentralization and school improvement* (pp. 84-101). San Francisco: Jossey-Bass.

Lewis, O. (1951). *Life in a Mexican village: Tepoztlan restudied.* Urbana: University of Illinois Press.

Lightfoot, S. (1984). *The good high school.* New York: Basic Books.

Little J. (1993). Professional community in comprehensive high schools. In J. Little & M. McLaughlin (Eds), *Teachers' Work* (pp. 137-163). New York: Teachers College Press.

Little, J., & McLaughlin, M. W. (1993). *Teachers' work.* New York: Teachers College Press.

Lomotey, K. (Ed.). (1990). *Going to school: The African-American experience.* Albany: State University of New York Press.

Lortie, D. C. (1975). *Schoolteacher: A sociological study.* Chicago: University of Chicago Press.

Lutz, F., & Merz, C. (1992). *The politics of school community relations.* New York: Teachers College Press.

Lutz, F. W., & Iannacone, L. (1978). *Public participation in local school districts.* Lexington, MA: D. C. Heath.

Malen, B., & Ogawa, R. T. (1988). Professional-patron influence on site-based governance councils: A confounding case study. *Educational Evaluation and Policy Analysis, 10,* 251-270.

Malen, B., Ogawa, R. T., & Kranz, J. (1990). What do we know about school-based management? A case study of the literature—a call for research. In W. H. Clune & J. F. Witte (Eds.), *Choice and control in American education, volume 2: The practice of choice, decentralization and school restructuring* (pp. 289-342). New York: Falmer Press.

Mannan, G., & Blackwell, J. (1992). Parent involvement: Barriers and opportunities. *The Urban Review, 24,* 219–226.

March, J. (1988). *Decisions and organizations.* New York: Basil Blackwell.

McLaren, P. (1993). Multiculturalism and the postmodern critique: Towards a pedagogy of resistance and transformation. *Cultural Studies, 7*(1), pp. 118–146.

McLaughlin, M. (1991, April). *Strategic sites for teachers' professional development.* Paper presented to annual meeting of the American Educational Research Association, Chicago.

McLaughlin, M. (1993). What matters most in teachers' workplace context? In J. Little & M. McLaughlin (Eds.), *Teachers' work.* New York: Teachers College Press.

McLaughlin, M. W., & Talbert, J. (1990). Constructing a personalized school environment. *Phi Delta Kappan, 72,* 230–235.

McMillan, D., & Chavis, D. (1986). Sense of community: A definition and theory. *Journal of Community Psychology, 14,* 6–23.

Meier, D. (1991). The kindergarten tradition in high school. In D. Jervis & C. Montag (Eds.), *Progressive education for the 1990s: Transforming practice.* New York: Teachers College Press.

Meier, D. (1995). *The power of their ideas.* Boston: Beacon Press.

Melaville, A. I., & Blank, M. J. (1991). *What it takes: Structuring interagency partnerships to connect children and families with comprehensive services.* Washington, DC: Education and Human Services Consortium.

Melaville, A. I., & Blank, M. J. (1993). *Together we can.* Washington, DC: U.S. Government Printing Office.

Mickelson, R. A., Yon, M. G., & Carlton-LaNey, I. (1995). Slipping through the cracks: The education of homeless children. In L. C. Rigsby, M. C. Reynolds, & M. C. Wang (Eds.), *School-community connections: Exploring issues for research and practice* (pp. 357–393). San Francisco: Jossey-Bass.

Mitchell, B. (1990). Loss, belonging and becoming: social policy themes for children and schools. In B. Mitchell & L. Cunningham (Eds.), *Educational leadership and the changing contexts of families, communities and schools: Eighty-ninth Yearbook of the National Society for the Study of Education* (pp. 19–51). Chicago: University of Chicago Press.

Moore, D. R. (1990). Voice and choice in Chicago. In W. H. Clune & J. F. Witte (Eds.), *Choice and control in American education, volume 2: The practice of choice, decentralization and school restructuring* (pp. 153–198). New York: Falmer Press.

Murphy, J., & Beck, L. G. (1995). *School-based management as school reform: Taking stock.* Thousand Oaks, CA: Corwin Press.

National Commission on Excellence in Education. (1983). *A nation at risk: The imperative for educational reform.* Washington, DC: U.S. Government Printing Office.

Newmann, F., & Wehlage, G. (1995). *Successful school restructuring.* Madison: Wisconsin Center for Educational Research.

Noddings, N. (1984). *Caring: A feminine approach to ethics and moral education.* Berkeley: University of California Press.

Noddings, N. (1992). *The challenge to care in schools.* New York: Teachers College Press.

O'Toole, K. (1995, Fall). James March: Should higher education be more efficient? *Stanford Educator,* pp. 3, 5, 12.

Parsons, T. (1937). *The structure of social action.* New York: McGraw-Hill.

Parsons, T. (1954). *Essays in sociological theory.* Glencoe, IL: The Free Press.

Perrow, C. (1970). *Organizational analysis: A sociological view.* Belmont, CA: Wadsworth.

Peshkin, A. (1995). The complex world of an embedded institution: Schools and their constituent publics. In L. C. Rigsby, M. C. Reynolds, & M. C. Wang (Eds.), *School-community connections: Exploring issues for research and practice* (pp. 229-258). San Francisco: Jossey-Bass.

Purkey, S. C., & Smith, M. S. (1983). Effective schools: A review. *Elementary School Journal, 83,* 427-452.

Putnam, D. (1995). Bowling alone. *Journal of Democracy, 6*(1), 7-14.

Quandt, J. (1970). *From small town to the great community.* New Brunswick, NJ: Rutgers University Press.

Redfield, R. (1941). *The folk culture of the Yucatan.* Chicago: University of Chicago Press.

Redfield, R. (1950). *A village that chose progress.* Chicago: University of Chicago Press.

Redfield, R. (1955). *The little community.* Uppsala, Sweden: Almquist and Wiksells.

Reyes, P. (1994, October). *Cultural citizenship and social responsibility: A call for change in educational administration. UCEA presidential address, 1993.* Presented at the annual conference of the University Council for Educational Administration, Houston, TX.

Rigsby, L. C. (1995). Introduction. In L. C. Rigsby, M. C. Reynolds, & M. C. Wang (Eds.), *School-community connections: Exploring issues for research and practice* (pp. 1-18). San Francisco: Jossey-Bass.

Rowan, B. (1990). Commitment and control: Alternative strategies for the organizational design of schools. *Review of Research in Education, 16,* 353-385.

Rutter, M., Maughan, B., Mortimore, P., Ouston, J., & Smith, A. (1979). *Fifteen thousand hours: Secondary schools and their effects on children.* Cambridge: Harvard University Press.

Sandel, M. (1996). America's search for a new public philosophy. *The Atlantic Monthly, 277,* 57-74.

Sarason, S. B. (1982). *The culture of the school and the problem of change.* Boston: Allyn and Bacon.

Sarason, S. B. (1990). *The predictable failure of educational reform.* San Francisco: Jossey-Bass.

Schlesinger, A. (1992). *The disuniting of America.* New York: W. W. Norton and Company.

Sergiovanni, T. (1992). *Moral leadership*. San Francisco: Jossey-Bass.

Sergiovanni, T. (1994). *Building community in schools*. San Francisco: Jossey-Bass.

Simmel, G. (1950). *The sociology of Georg Simmel* (K. Wolff, Ed. & Trans.). Glencoe, IL: The Free Press. (Original work published 1903)

Sizer, T. (1984). *Horace's compromise*. Boston: Houghton Mifflin.

Slater, R. O., Bolman, L., Crow, G. M., Goldring, E., & Thurston, P. W. (1994). Leadership and management processes: Taxonomy and overview. In W. K. Hoy (Ed.), *Educational administration: The UCEA document base*. New York: McGraw-Hill.

Slattery, P. (1995). *Curriculum development in the postmodern era*. New York: Garland Publishing.

Smrekar, C. (1996). The Kentucky family resource centers: The challenges of remaking family-school interactions. In J. Cibulka & W. Kritek (Eds.), *Coordination among schools, families and communities: Prospects for educational reform* (pp. 3–25). Albany: State University of New York Press.

Solomon, D., & Kendall, A. J. (1979). *Children in classrooms: An investigation of person-environment interaction*. New York: Praeger.

Swap, S. M. (1993). *Developing home-school partnerships: From concepts to practice*. New York: Teachers College Press.

Tönnies, F. (1957). *Community and Society* (Charles Loomis, Ed. & Trans.). East Lansing: Michigan State University Press. (Original work published as *Gemeinschaft und Gesellschaft*, 1887)

Toqueville, A. (1945). *Democracy in America*. (H. Reeve, Trans., & P. Bradley, Ed.). New York: Vintage Books. (Original work published 1835)

Tyack, D. (1974). *The one best system*. Cambridge: Harvard University Press.

Tyack, D. (1990). "Restructuring" in historical perspective. *Teachers College Record, 92*(2), 170–191.

Tyack, D. B., & Hansot, E. (1982). *Managers of virtue: Public school leadership in America, 1820–1980*. New York: Basic Books.

Wagstaff, L. H., & Gallagher, K. S. (1990). Families, communities, and educational leadership. In L. Cunningham & B. Mitchell (Eds.), *Educational leadership and changing contexts in families, communities, and schools: Eighty-ninth yearbook of the national society for the study of education* (pp. 91–117). Chicago: University of Chicago Press.

Walberg, H., & Walberg, H., III. (1994). Losing local control. *Educational Researcher, 23*(5), 19–26.

Wang, M. C., Haertel, G. D., & Walberg, H. J. (1995). The effectiveness of collaborative school-linked services. In L. C. Rigsby, M. C. Reynolds, & M. C. Wang (Eds.), *School-community connections: Exploring issues for research and practice* (pp. 283–309). San Francisco: Jossey-Bass.

Weber, M. (1947). *The theory of social and economic organization* (E. M. Henderson & T. Parsons, Trans.). New York: The Free Press. (Original work published 1925)

Weise, R., & Murphy, J. (1995a). SBM in historical perspective, 1900–1950. In J.

Murphy & L. G. Beck (Eds.), *School-based management as school reform: Taking stock* (pp. 93–115). Thousand Oaks, CA: Corwin Press.

Weise, R., & Murphy, J. (1995b). SBM in historical perspective: The community control movement, 1965–1975. In J. Murphy & L. G. Beck (Eds.), *School-based management as school reform: Taking stock* (pp. 116–130). Thousand Oaks, CA: Corwin Press.

West, C. (1993). *Race matters.* Boston: Beacon Press.

White, W. A. (1994). California's state partnership for school-linked services. In L. Adler & S. Gardner (Eds.), *The politics of linking schools and social services* (pp. 171–178). Washington, DC: The Falmer Press.

Wirth, L. (1970). Urbanism as a way of life. In R. Gutman & D. Popenoe (Eds.), *Neighborhood, city and metropolis* (pp. 54–68). New York: Random House. (Original work published 1938)

Wohlstetter, P., & Odden, A. (1992). Rethinking school-based management policy and research. *Educational Administration Quarterly, 28,* 529–549.

Young, I. (1986). The ideal of community and the politics of difference. *Social Theory and Practice, 12*(1), 1–25.

Index

About the Authors

Carol Merz is Dean of the School of Education at the University of Puget Sound since 1986. She holds a B.A. and M.A. from Stanford University and a doctorate from Washington State University. She has been a classroom teacher and administrator in California and Washington. Her interests are in educational policy and politics. She previously co-authored *The Politics of School Community Relations* with Frank Lutz.

Gail C. Furman is an Associate Professor of Education in the Department of Educational Leadership at Washington State University and serves as Program Coordinator at WSU's Tri-Cities campus. Dr. Furman received her B.A. from George Mason University, her M.A. from Radford University, and her Ph.D. in Educational Adminstration from Washington State University. Her specialty areas are educational reform policy and qualitative research methodology.